The Spirit
of a Woman

Stories to Empower and Inspire

SANTA
MONICA
PRESS

Published by: Santa Monica Press LLC
P.O. Box 1076
Santa Monica, CA 90406-1076
1-800-784-9553
www.santamonicapress.com
books@santamonicapress.com

Printed in the United States

Santa Monica Press books are available at special quantity discounts when purchased in bulk by corporations, organizations, or groups. Please call our Special Sales department at 1-800-784-9553.

This book is intended to provide general information. The publisher, author, distributor, and copyright owner are not engaged in rendering health, medical, legal, financial, or other professional advice or services. The publisher, author, distributor, and copyright owner are not liable or responsible to any person or group with respect to any loss, illness, or injury caused or alleged to be caused by the information found in this book.

ISBN-13 978-1-59580-052-7

Library of Congress Cataloging-in-Publication Data

The spirit of a woman : stories to empower and inspire / edited by Terry László-Gopadze ; foreword by Angeles Arrien.
    p. cm.
ISBN 978-1-59580-052-7
1. Women—Psychology. 2. Women heroes. 3. Role models. 4. Women and literature. 5. Creation (Literary, artistic, etc.) I. László-Gopadze, Terry.
HQ1206.S685 2010
155.3'33—dc22
                              2010002727

Cover and interior design and production by Future Studio
Cover and interior art by Nichola Moss (www.nicholart.com)

"Caught Sight of Angels," from Sparkles and Shadows by Suni Paz, copyright © 2007 Elsa Calandrelli, pseudonym Suni Paz. Used by permission of Suni Paz, Del Sol Books.

Mixed Sources
Product group from well-managed forests and other controlled sources
www.fsc.org Cert no. SW-COC-002283
© 1996 Forest Stewardship Council
FSC

The Spirit of a Woman

Stories to Empower and Inspire

Edited by Terry László-Gopadze
Foreword by Angeles Arrien
Artwork by Nichola Moss

For all the women who have come into my life
and changed it story by story,
and
for my faithful husband Lee and my son Paul,
who gave me the home and wings to live my dreams.

In a poem, Wendell Berry says, "Be joyful though you have considered all of the facts." Spirit within is a source of renewable joy for us no matter what the exterior circumstances are. Spirit within, by whatever name or experience we call it, is our wellspring when the going gets tough. Inner life with spirit is not a holy retreat from life's difficulty, but it is our comfort, strength, and joy in the midst of life.

—SALLY MAHÉ and KATHY COVERT,
A Greater Democracy Day by Day

Contents

Foreword

Angeles Arrien

*The Great Spirit must have loved stories because the
Great Spirit made a lot of people.*

—INUIT PROVERB

The Spirit of a Woman is a compelling and uplifting anthology filled with inspirational and
empowering true stories from women from
many different professions, faiths, and cultures. Terry
László-Gopadze has assembled these stories into powerful themes and chapters that are relevant for our
times: how to make changes and choices; foster connections and independence; honor the gifts of courage
and challenge; and trust the relationship of Destiny to
Faith and divine intervention. This anthology speaks

very powerfully to the internal and external Muses in our life that either release or ignite the unlimited depths of the feminine principle within every human being, whether male or female.

At different times in history, certain archetypal collective images, myths, and stories tend to emerge and recede again—in response not only to evolutionary processes, but also to the spiritual needs of human kind. According to psychologist Carl Jung, there exists in the collective unconscious a clear tendency to understand dualities and paradoxes—especially the poles of good and evil, which have split too far apart in our time. Jung felt that the needed reconciliation could only come through an intermediary, which he believed to be the neglected feminine principle found both in men and women.

Additionally, he believed that the Muses were the emergent images that could assist us most in claiming the neglected feminine principle. In Greek mythology, all nine Muses are divine forces in the form of women that guide us in the making and remaking of the human spirit in the world. Each one calls us to a path of creativity and commitment to live an authentic life. William Butler Yeats described the Muses' mandate in the terse phrase: "To speak of one's emotions without fear or moral ambition, to come out from under the shadow of men's minds, to forget their needs, to be utterly oneself, that is all the Muses care for."

Relentlessly the Muses call forth our authenticity and gifts and talents. All nine of these mythical women inspire us to create our futures and to meet our destinies. They compel us to take up our own soul tasks; and require us to bring our authentic natures to earth.

The Spirit of a Woman contains true stories, all by women, who have been deeply touched by their own muse. Their stories show the courage, compassion, authenticity, and forgiveness that are required to live and come from the healthy feminine principle. Each one demonstrates depth, self-knowledge, and the ability to bridge both the internal and external worlds. The range of these stories reveals our interconnectedness and brings us together into a global community—from Josefina Burgos's story of imprisonment and torture in Chile; to Hagit Ra'anan's story as an Israeli woman coming to peace with the Palestinians after her husband had been killed by one; and to lessons learned by S. Kelley Harrell through her part-Cherokee grandfather, who tended to bee hives, and listened to the ways and messages of the bees. Even though these sample stories seem to be very diverse, every story within this anthology has a special and consistent quality of conviction, love, care, faith, wit, resourcefulness, and humility. Without a doubt, this is the best collection of stories to date that honors and illustrates the power, beauty, and integrity of the feminine principle that resides in each human being.

Carl Jung further proposed that the reclaimed feminine principle would create the intermediary bridge needed to reconcile the existing human needs and collective learning surrounding the unsolved conflicts, dualities, polarities, and oppositions present within the human psyche. He saw Pegasus, the winged horse—much favored by the Muses—as a bridging symbol for the positive instinctual force of the subconscious that signals the unification, or synthesis, of polarities and oppositions. Pegasus comes from the Greek word *pegae*, which means "geyser," or "to draw forth water." The essential symbol for the feminine has long been water, *aqua femina*. Whenever hooves of Pegasus drew water, the Muses would always appear. Many have said that those who drink from the mysterious waters are endowed with poetic inspiration, loving expression, and heightened creativity.

The feminine principle symbolized by the Muses and the positive instinctual force of the subconscious revealed by Pegasus are the creative emissaries that can assist us in discovering solutions that can support and move us forward individually and collectively. Our unobstructed creativity is the ambassador, connected to the mystery, that allows us to release the courage, vision, wisdom, and love needed to create a future world that works for everybody.

The Spirit of a Woman demonstrates three major aspects of the feminine principle:

- any contribution coming from care and love contributes to the development of the human enterprise;

- fully trusting our own intuition and guidance, even when it goes against established norms, is a courageous act of integrity; and

• commitment of meaningful action, service, work, or creativity makes a real difference both individually and collectively.

This extraordinary collection of stories, put together by Terry László-Gopadze, demonstrates the power of the feminine principle in action, and shows us how it can, and does, change the world. It is impossible to read these stories without having your estimation of the human spirit rise, and to experience the deep living feminine principle globally residing in Mother Earth in *aqua femina*—the deep waters and oceans that embrace Mother Earth—and in our own natures at this time in history. What committed actions will you take to foster the feminine principle within your own nature and in the world as a result of reading these exceptional stories?

Angeles Arrien is an award-winning author, educator, and cultural anthropologist. She is the founder and president of the Angeles Arrien Foundation for Cross-Cultural Education and Research and author of many books, including *The Four-Fold Way* and *The Second Half of Life*.

Introduction

I invite you to experience *The Spirit of a Woman* as a spiritual gift.

It is filled with stories of the individual, mystical experiences that empower women to travel a spiritual pathway, no matter what difficulties they may encounter. Every woman's story is unique. The power of her story comes from belief in a larger world of possibilities that is relevant and sustaining.

I honor women who have the inner spirit to face challenges, to go into the dark and emerge with compassion and truth. I am inspired by women who confront their fears and rally the strength of their hearts to find meaning and faith. I respect women who journey into the depths of confusion and emerge with love and healing. I applaud them.

My own experience with facing the "unfaceable" has blessed me with a kind of freedom. A cancer diagnosis, black and fearful as it was, ultimately brought healing into my life. Contemplating my own death initiated a dark period in my life. I sought solitude so that

I could heal my body, my mind, and my spirit. My old ideas of God were cast aside, and I opened to finding God in everyone and everything, even in my diagnosis of cancer. Paying attention to my heart and intuition, I encountered many dimensions of spirit.

My prayers were answered by women who came into my life to mentor me. They shared the stories of their journeys of healing and growth, and in so doing, they showed me the framework of a new way of life. Awakening slowly, little-by-little, day-by-day, I came to a new life enriched by spiritual dimensions.

Am I unusual? No. All women are naturally gifted with the power to create, overcome, and transform. They trust their wisdom and, with body and spirit, they find their way in the dark. There is always a moment within a crisis when one feels connected to spirit and knows it is possible to rise out of the ashes alive and whole. To witness this kind of transcendence is to understand that what is human is holy. There is no separation.

I am blessed to live by the sea in California. Some time ago, on a beautiful, sunny day after many gray, overcast ones, I went to a yoga class. Months of health problems were diminishing and I felt well. As I left the class and walked through a garden, I experienced a magical moment and rejoiced in simply being alive. Suddenly, I was aware of butterflies around me, perhaps as many as fifty. In my happiness, I thought, "The butterflies mean change and freedom, and their message is for me!"

As I passed through the garden gate, I mused that the butterflies had already survived several life cycles and were surely telling me that everything can be right in the world.

Moments later, I stepped into a shop where a young woman greeted me. Her face showed stress, but her voice was optimistic.

"Did you see the butterflies?" she asked. "I think they mean abundance. Oh, I hope they do. I'm so worried about money, but I think they are here to tell me not to worry any more."

I wanted to share what the butterflies had meant to me, and I almost began my story, but then I stopped. *She* needed to be heard. She needed me to be with *her*, to hear her.

Leaving that shop, I drove around the corner to another store where I was greeted by a handsome young man wearing his best salesman smile. We walked through his shop into a courtyard to look at the fountains and benches that he had for sale, but my focus that day was on the butterflies. Many more were in the courtyard, and I couldn't contain myself.

"Look! See the butterflies? They are a sign of something good in your life," I told him.

"I'm open to that," he said. "But I think they're moths."

As more butterflies filled the space around us, I just knew I could convince him. "No, look! They are butterflies."

He looked me in the eye, sans salesman smile

this time.

"I think they're moths."

I walked to my car smiling, glad to have encountered each of the young people. Moths and butterflies both have a place in the world. We can be open
to their significance, whatever it is for each of us. We
can listen and allow a voice for all beliefs. Each voice
and each belief brings us closer to the many faces of
God.

Stories of transformation and hope remind us
that we have freedom to choose. We can choose to be
authentic, to follow our rhythms, to speak our truths,
and to be faithful. We can choose whom we love and
the way we perceive our world and ultimately our god
. . . or gods.

The idea for this book was born as I sat beside
a hospital bed. My father had fallen while walking his
dog. Waiting for and fearing test results, I read to him.
I wanted to create good memories even as we shared
anxious hours of uncertainty about his future. Other
times of distress had taught me that when disaster
threatened, it helped to create a sanctuary that would
sustain me as my own resources became exhausted.

The waiting ended when a doctor came to tell
my father that he would have to undergo brain surgery
to remove a blood clot that had formed as a conse-
quence of the fall. The doctor's message meant that the
treadmill of hospital admissions and departures during
recent years had not ended yet. Concern for my father
caused me to weep.

But when I searched my father's face, he just smiled. His courage in being ready to go wherever his life led him didn't remove my anguish, but it dried my tears and refocused our connection to each other. We were then able to enjoy what we had in the moment.

Still sitting beside his bed as he slept after the surgery, I wrote the outline and the premise for this book. The idea of sharing stories of spiritual power was born out of struggles with my health problems, grief for my desperately ill father, and sadness over my mother's recent placement in a nursing home. We all must confront difficulties, sometimes many at once. We all must face challenges that have no simple solutions. Our salvation lies in going beyond the limits of everyday existence. Challenges can become opportunities to reach into our souls and find meaning. Somehow, we can hold fast to hope, goodness, and beauty as we live through grief-stricken and debilitating days. During my own dark days, I was able to choose.

In that spirit, I offer you these stories of women discovering the sacred. Collecting them has changed my life in profound ways; each story increased my faith and taught me that spirit is always present in our lives.

Now I wait with an open heart and I listen to the women who enter my life. It is a privilege to receive their choices, their desires, their dreams, and their pain. Most often, I am silent so their music can play.

A Catholic priest recently said it this way: "Every individual has a unique story. To reject that story is to reject the person. To accept it is to embrace that person." A story is a spiritual gift. To really listen to the story of another is a spiritual practice.

The following stories are raw and revealing. They are imperfect, quirky, tender, and harrowing. They mirror the lives of the women who tell them. Embrace them and rejoice in the spirit of all women and the power of their stories.

ONE

Connections

If we have no peace, it is because we have forgotten that we belong to each other.

—MOTHER TERESA,
Love: A Fruit Always in Season

Every heart is the other heart. Every soul is the other soul. Every face is the other face. The individual is the one illusion.

—MARGUERITE YOUNG,
Miss MacIntosh, My Darling

Every person we encounter has a meaning and a purpose. Enlightenment emerges from the personal connections of our everyday lives. We are all connected to each other in an intricate and delicate web that holds out never-ending opportunities to live in peace, forgiveness, healing, and harmony. We have the vast capacity to move beyond our fears, resentments, and limited beliefs, which only diminish us. We create new visions when we come from a place of joy, gratitude, and service to others.

The great courage and wisdom in the following stories inspire us to remember our interdependence. Each woman deals with loss in a way that creates more love and unity with others, and peace within herself. Each woman defines her own destiny and authenticity. As each one lets go of the past, we reap her transcendence, her insights, and her blessings. These women understand the power of compassion to reveal the eternal to us, and to help us see it in everyone else. The stories enchant us and we realize that we all create our days. . . .

A Storycatcher Is Born

Christina Baldwin

Life hangs on a narrative thread.
This thread is a braid of stories that inform us about who
    we are,
and where we come from, and where we might go.
The thread is slender but strong:
We trust it to hold us
and allow us to swing over the edge of the known
into the future we dream first in words.

I'm ten years old in this moment, home from school and scrunched on elbows and knees reading the afternoon newspaper that I have brought in from the mailbox and laid out on the living room carpet. I push my straight brown hair behind my ears and enjoy a glass of milk and some snack my mother has prepared. Reading headlines is a new daily ritual, for in fourth grade, teachers are starting to talk about the world beyond Beacon Heights Elementary at the suburban edge of Minneapolis.

Today, this is a daily ritual that will go very differently.

In a supportive progression of awareness, children awake to the world around them in concentric circles: first their families, then playmates and other families, then their neighborhood, school, the town or city they live in, the country in which they reside, and the wider world beyond. Children ask an unending series of evolving questions designed to map their sense of place in the order of things: "How do babies get here?" "Why is Jerrod a boy and I'm not?" "Do all people believe in God?" "Why did we move to Minnesota?" These questions become universal life-long themes: "Who am I?" "With whom do I belong?" "What do I believe about the nature of human beings?" "What power might I exercise in the world around me, and who will support or undermine what I think I can do?"

In this moment when I am ten, two stories run in parallel columns across the front page of the *Minneapolis Star*. There is famine in India, people are hungry, starving, wandering in search of food; there is surplus grain in the United States, a bumper crop overfilling the silos, leaving trains of corn and wheat parked on the spur lines at the edge of farm towns. Like a bolt of lightning going through my mind, these two stories come together; too much food here, not enough food there, and the solution: ship the "too much" to the place where there is "not enough." I sit upright, absorbing my insight. *Why haven't the adults thought of this? It's so obvious!* Many thoughts are firing through me simultaneously: excitement at the ease and applicability of my idea, eagerness to set this plan in motion, belief that my father, soon due home from work, will know how to help me.

When children are adequately cared for, they experience a supportive progression of evidence in their ability to influence their environment. When a baby cries and parents respond, action and reaction become the first healthy lessons in life. Later, they learn to negotiate with other children, to test limits and learn, both through experience and vicariously through watching others and listening to stories of success and failure. Like questions, experiences of personal power extend in concentric circles into the micro-communities that surround childhood. I was a child who had been tended well enough for self-assurance to flourish. I was ready to meet the world, to test myself beyond the borders of my tiny suburban life.

I sit by the paper in reverie and see myself launching ships full of grain out of San Francisco harbor—a little white girl from Minnesota who has been invited to this moment because it was her great idea. I swing back my arm and slam a bottle of champagne against the prow. The ship slides into the water . . .

and then there is magic, for I see, on the other side of the world, a little brown girl who stands with empty, outspread arms welcoming the first of the rescue vessels. She and her family will eat bread tonight because I thought of this; because we are connected; because I get it that the world is both big and small; because every person can make a difference, can put an idea into action and make things better.

In this moment, boundaries blur. I become the girl who is fed *and* the girl who is hungry. I become the grain and the pestle on the grinding stone. I become the mother kneading the dough, the fire that cooks, and the hungry mouth that takes the bread. I have no name for this melding, nor any need to explain it. I sit entranced with a sense that my soul may actually consist of many parts, that "I" am a loaf broken into pieces, charged with this exact discovery: to claim our wholeness. Time and place are lost, and the afternoon sun ceases to bang at the picture window of my familiar home.

The brown girl and I are sitting somewhere. It is warm, and the ground is packed hard. We face each other. I extend my white and lightly freckled arm; she extends her brown arm. I look into her almost-black and fathomless eyes; she looks into my brown-flecked hazel eyes. I touch her black and shiny braid; she touches my short brown silk. She smells of dust and spices; I smell of chalkboard and newspaper ink. As she becomes real, I become somehow more real. I offer my glass of milk, my mother's homemade cookies. She accepts tentatively, and then eats ravenously.

Somehow, I know her story and she knows mine.

And then my father comes home.

Looking back, I wonder what I expected him to do. Something along the lines of calling President Eisenhower and being my voice of authority, the proud dad announcing, "Don't worry, Mr. President, Chrissie Baldwin has this figured out. . . ." That's not the call he made. He was and is my hero, this daddy. A conscientious objector in World War II, I had watched him stand for unpopular causes and articulate his values. But this day, he must have been tired and what he passes on to me is resignation. He is thirty-five, working a low-level job to support his wife and four small children. His dream of being a sociology professor has withered under the challenge of facing the McCarthy era and the Cold War without a veteran's record.

My parents had raised me around a huge subsistence garden, where I had developed a rudimentary understanding of harvest, abundance, food preservation, and eating out of the pantry all winter. I thought I understood how the world worked, and I thought I could take our garden model and lay it over the world's needs. We sat on the couch and after I explained to him what needed to be done, he explained to me the economics of price fixing, commodities futures, and farm subsidies. "I'm sorry," he said, "there's nothing you can do."

The ten-year-old goes into shock. My spell is broken, and my heart, and my connection to my other self. The brown girl is falling away from me, her mouth round with a silent cry. My grief is huge and unexplainable. I turn to anger—surely the world cannot be like this! It cannot! Late that night, when I am sure no one can hear me, I cry inconsolably into my pillow, begging her forgiveness. And I make a life decision: I want to change the world. I want my life to count in a good way. I want to be used by history.

Heroic models, then and now, are stories of people who step into the gap; whose actions turn the tide; who pluck peace and good fortune from the jaws of disaster; who transform themselves in the crucible of crisis. For years, I would watch for the heroic moment to come for me in a dramatic way. I expected to be chosen—by God, or life—to be thrown into the maw of events, to lead the charge and storm the Bastille, to be called to India in search for my twin. Instead, a different kind of activism has been harvested out of me: to become a champion for story itself, to profoundly understand that story is the seed of our ability to love ourselves, each other, and anything else. We are the creatures who turn raw experience into words. Only through story do we comprehend what is happening to us, and choose to find our way. Word by word leads us to action by action. We are dependent on language to become fully human.

It's as though the divine said to me, "Heroes are everywhere. Your role is to notice and listen. Your role is to help people hear their own stories and learn. Your role is to help the community hear each other's stories. Story is a map: what gets one person through is a grid that gets another person through. Preserve the story. Hold that space, my daughter. And foster action that rises from story's wisdom." By age fourteen, I had started keeping a diary that has grown into a life-long record of my relationship with my own story. Journal writing has taught me that life experience has a capacity to transform into something much greater than the moment itself, and that our greatest moments have the potential to serve as sources of inspiration way beyond the influence of our own lives. But these moments need story. Experience needs to be worked through the grinding stone of words, submitted to the pestle of reflection, and connected to previous experiences—our own and others'—and then they can become the bread of life itself.

I notice when people practice random acts of kindness. I admire those who will not give up. I honor people who say yes and no at just the right moment, and act decisively as though everything they've ever lived through has prepared them. I cry and laugh at the goodness in our hearts, our willingness to offer the altruistic gesture—to climb a tree for someone else's cat, to stop and help a stranger, to rescue a child, or help an elder. And I find my greatest calling is to receive these tales in a sacred manner, to create spaces of attention that can hold them. The art of storycatching is round; it is both listening and telling. So I also do my best to serve as the bard, the town crier, the medicine woman, the Storycatcher who holds up the mirror of human goodness so we can believe in each other anew.

What truly happened for me that day over fifty years ago was that I entered the story. I became all the characters. I became the scene and the world that held it. I became the conditions in which the girl lived and I lived, and the power of storycatching enthralled me. I have marched in protest, stood in witness, challenged authority, walked away from work that held no integrity, rebelled against the injustices that trap us all—and the greatest work I do is catch the story.

During the height of the Iraq war, a tiny middle-aged woman, who seemed barely able to see over the steering wheel, began driving a bright red Hummer around the little town where I now live. She was quite noticeable in an environment where many of my friends were buying hybrid cars, and we were all talking about reducing our carbon footprint. None of us knew this woman, but occasionally as we sat sipping lattes at one of our local coffeehouses, her presence would come up in conversation and we would scoff at her choice. "What can she be thinking? Why would any sensible person buy such a gas hog at this time?"

Good questions, I thought, and watched for an opportunity to catch her story. One day, I pulled into the grocery store parking lot and there she was—descending from the driver's seat of her Hummer. I parked in the empty slot next to her and said hello. "Pretty noticeable car," I commented in a voice that smiled. "I've seen you around and been wondering what attracted you to buy a Hummer?" I waited.

"My son is driving one of these in Iraq," she

said, stroking the fender with a mother's touch. "I know it's not logical, but I have this fantasy—if I stay safe in mine, he'll stay safe in his. . . ." Tears welled up in her eyes and in mine.

"It's hard to know what to do, isn't it?" She nods, I go on. "A bunch of my friends and I stand at the intersection once a month with Women in Black— maybe you've seen us—a long row, in silence, everyone dressed in black clothes. It's a movement started between Israeli and Palestinian women to reach across that war, to say simply: we want peace."

She stiffens slightly. "I support the troops. . . ."

"Of course you do. So do I. Think about it." We walk into the store. "May I share your story about the Hummer . . . and your son?" I ask.

She grabs a cart. "Sure. The more people thinking of him—thinking of all of them—that's good, isn't it?" This time I nod. She heads for the deli. I aim toward produce. I wouldn't recognize her if I saw her again, so I can't ask how she's doing. It's been over several years since I've seen the red Hummer.

Story links lives. Amid the ravages of war, story connects us across what first appear to be divisions and differences. There is a little door between people that opens to our stories. When we are distracted or judgmental, we rush by this door without noticing. But when we slow down, when we look in each other's eyes and let curiosity arise, we can knock gently and be treated to a moment of recognition that will change our hearts for a long time. This interaction in the parking lot lasted perhaps two minutes, but I have told our story to people on three continents. We made a little bit of world peace in that parking lot—and I found another face of my twin.

Most of what we know about being human comes from stories of being human. Anthropologist Laurens van der Post believed ninety percent of accumulated knowledge, wisdom, socialization, encouragement, or discouragement has been passed through uncounted generations by story after story. When the power of story shows up at the fire, or comes into the room, it can move us to hatred or love with words alone—we choose. Over and over, we have destroyed or saved ourselves based on what stories we have chosen to guide us. I believe we have again come to a point where our ability to save or destroy ourselves largely depends on the stories we tell each other.

Are we really so different? Is it worth killing each other over the spices of our diversity? Is anything so important that we should destroy the health of the planet? Stories lead us to action, or bind us to inaction. Stories define what we pay attention to, or ignore. In a crisis of such proportion as the times we live in, there are no idle stories: Every tale we tell, listen to, or believe has impact. In thousands of languages, in every corner of the earth, story is at work. The question is: Will we work with story? If we want a better world, we need to tell stories that move us in the direction of our hope, and lead us to actions that create that world. We need to donate the seemingly insignificant and ordinary interactions of our lives to the grinding stone of insight and make them into stories that inspire, inform, and activate the best that is in us. Then we can change the world. The story is the map.

I am sixty-plus years old in this moment. An old brown woman and I are sitting somewhere. It is on warm, packed ground. We face each other. Our skin is wrinkled. The palms of her hands are worn by time; veins ride on the back of my finger bones. I look into her almost-black and fathomless eyes; she looks into my brown-flecked hazel eyes. I touch her white and frazzled braid; she touches my gray-streaked, shoulder-length hair. She smells of hot sun and curry; I smell of coming rain. As she is real, I am real. She offers me a cup of chai. We share a piece of bread. We spin the Storycatcher's web. The world holds together another day.

No Apologies Necessary

Colleen Haggerty

That only which we have within, can we see without. If we meet no gods, it is because we harbor none.
—RALPH WALDO EMERSON,
The Conduct of Life

He never said he was sorry.

Fifteen years had passed since the accident that took my left leg. He was the driver of the car that pinned me against our car, ripping away my leg. And now, it suddenly dawned on me, with all the power of a sledgehammer, that he had never said he was sorry.

Two years after the accident, during the trial seeking compensation for my loss, he and I weren't allowed to speak to each other. But I watched this big bear of a man walk into the courtroom and sit with his lawyer at the table to my left, hunched over, eyes cast down, peering at me briefly, then looking away shamefully. I felt sorry for him; I always had. I would never want to trade places with him. How could I live with myself if I knew I was responsible for dismembering another human being? I definitely got the better end of the deal. But there he was, being who I imagined I would be if I were in his shoes. Whispers around the courtroom informed me that he had ulcers and other physical maladies resulting from the stress of it all. Good.

But he never said he was sorry.

Every year in early January, I would fall into the depths of depression and contemplation as I neared the anniversary of the accident. I never felt joy at having survived. I never experienced the elation of a second chance at life. I felt only loneliness and despair.

He never said he was sorry.

On this fifteenth anniversary, something snapped as I sat in my living room waiting for the phone call I didn't know I was waiting for. Like an unexpected punch to the gut, I realized that he had never contacted me to be sure I'm OK. He'd never written a nice note of apology for ruining my life. He'd never driven down to see me to make sure that I'm real and not a recurring nightmare. So I decided to call him; I'd show him what a nightmare is.

I called directory assistance to get his number

in Victoria, British Columbia, where I knew he lived. They only had his mother's number, so I called her. I didn't know if she was aware that her son had ripped away a young women's leg, so I just left my name and number and asked her to have him contact me.

The next day, it dawned on me: he might not remember me. Does he even know what yesterday was? Does he know my name? Would he even call me or would he ignore this plea for connection? I was afraid I'd embarrass myself by having to explain what he did to me before I yelled at him for doing it.

After all, he never said he was sorry.

By the time I got home from work the next day, I felt extremely nervous. Anxiously waiting for his call, I paced and smoked, smoked and paced. And then the phone rang.

"Hello?"

His slight accent responded, "Hello, Colleen. This is Harvey."

"Do you remember who I am?" I demanded.

Through his sobs, he responded, "Oh yes."

Accusingly, I pleaded, "Do you know what yesterday was?"

"Oh yes, and I think of you every year. I think of you all the time," he cried.

What was he doing, crying like that? How can I get mad at him now? I didn't know if I'd hear from him, so I hadn't mentally written my script. He said, "I'm sorry," a lot, but this wasn't going like I wanted. His willingness to apologize took away my steam.

We agreed to meet in Victoria. He still hadn't traveled the road of the accident, so coming to Seattle would be too difficult for him. Too difficult? Because I went to college near the accident site, I traveled that road countless times. Each time I drove by the spot, my mouth would salivate with the metallic taste of shock. Sometimes I'd cry; sometimes I'd allow the conversation to carry on with the person with whom I was driving, pretending it was just like any other piece of roadway; sometimes I'd cover up any feelings by lighting up another cigarette. Too difficult? He doesn't know what difficult is.

In preparation for our meeting, I spent five therapy sessions with my newest, and most effective, therapist, realizing how angry I was at Harvey. My anger at what happened to me had never been this directed before. I had spent fifteen years pushing down the lid on this boiling concoction of anger, grief, and sadness. The daily stabbing phantom pains in my missing leg offered ample opportunity to push this anger further into the pot. When I would least expect it, the stew would start its slow boil and begin to ooze out. The mere mention of taking a walk from my boyfriend would send me into an internal fury. *How far will we go? Will I be able to walk back without pain? Why does he assume I can do this?* I couldn't admit my limitations, my abnormality. I had to forge ahead like any other girlfriend would. Instead of expressing my anger, I'd yell at him for forgetting to lock the car door or not offering to carry the backpack. On those mornings when my prosthetic leg didn't fit well, the seething anger would swell in my gut and I'd throw the closest innocuous object I could find across the room. "Stupid leg maker," I'd grumble, "can't even make a *@#$ leg that fits right!" This flash of rage would pass through me, and I would storm out of my bedroom as fast as my altered gait would allow. Any time I felt the inadequacy of my limited body, I'd light up another cigarette to drown in the smokescreen of denial. It was a relief to finally target my anger where it belonged: at Harvey.

My brother Matthew and his boyfriend Kirk accompanied me to Victoria. We stayed at the Empress Hotel on Valentine's weekend. Harvey and I were to experience a unique kind of love that Valentine's Day.

We agreed to meet in the lobby of the hotel. At the appointed time, Matthew and Kirk walked with me, steadying me as we descended the ramp into the lobby. "Do you want us to stay until you find him?" Matthew asked. "No, I need to do this alone," I replied. They both gave me hugs of strength and slowly walked back up the ramp, glancing over their shoulders protectively. I peered back over mine for one last dose of encouragement. I felt as fierce as a lioness protecting her cub and as vulnerable as the cub itself. I imagined seeing Harvey and running up to him, even though I can't run, and hitting him repeatedly in the chest, screaming every profanity I could imagine. This fantasy of hitting and hitting and hitting was very consoling. I couldn't wait.

Armored by my anger, shaking from my fear,

I searched the lobby looking for a face I didn't really remember. A sea of people checking in for the weekend congested the room. I started feeling lightheaded as I scanned the crowd. Then I saw him, a big lug of a man, walking toward me. Oh, no . . . he's too big to hit. As he got closer I could see he was crying. Hey, aren't I the one who should be crying? He walked right up to me and asked for a hug. I'm hugging him. Wait. Stop the camera. It's not supposed to happen like this. When does the scene where I hit him and scream like a mad woman take place? What's happening here? Who wrote this syrupy little script?

We decided to take a walk in the hotel gardens. We spent hours walking and talking, first outside and then in the bar, drinking beer and smoking cigarettes. My resolve dissolved with the outpouring of words I never knew I needed to hear: "I've always thought about you," "When I see a young woman who looks like you, my day is ruined," "My life was devastated because of this," "My self-blame was so deep; I spent a year in counseling."

OK, now that one got me. . . . A simple year and he had it all wrapped up? I've been to four counselors over the fifteen years and I'm still wondering what's keeping me from being happy. But aside from that comment, my anger started to subside.

We talked about his life and how severely altered it was because of the accident. Any time the reality of what happened hit him, any time he saw a woman who looked like me, he became moody and mean.

"I became like Dr. Jekyll and Mr. Hyde: nice guy one minute and angry the next," he sobbed. I could see the pain and guilt in his tear-filled eyes. "My wife couldn't take it anymore. She finally divorced me."

"I replay the accident over and over and try to see what I would have done differently," he explained. His face contorted in anguish, expressing what I felt inside, but didn't have the heart to say. I didn't expect this. I thought this was going to be my show. Now I couldn't spill my guts and tell him how I question my attractiveness as a woman because I limp around with a plastic leg; how I have to mentally prepare myself for a simple walk around the neighborhood with my dog; how I feel so distant from others because they don't understand my pain. I couldn't paint the picture of what this looks like for me on a daily basis. His obvious guilt proved to me that he had been through enough.

"I'd give you my leg if I could," he offered.

"I don't want your leg, Harvey," I answered.

When I started college nine months after the accident, I played a game I hadn't played since I was a child. I pretended a fairy had given me three wishes. As I was walking through campus, my prosthetic leg rubbing painfully on my stump, the first thought was to wish for my leg back. I realized immediately, even in a fantasy world, that wasn't possible. In that moment, it dawned on me that this loss is a lifelong gig and it was up to me to learn from it.

During his year of counseling, Harvey discovered that what happened wasn't his fault, it was an accident. This was the nugget I left with. It was an accident. I always said, "I was in an accident, but it was Harvey's fault." That day, I came to understand that accidents don't assign fault, they just are. He and I reviewed the accident in detail. For the first time, we understood what happened from each other's perspective.

"Our car had spun out on the snowy freeway. When we came to a stop, we were facing traffic," I explained.

"Why were you out of the car?" he asked.

"No one was stopping to help us. I wanted to flag down some help. All the cars were driving slowly by us in the right lane; I thought for sure someone could help me stop traffic so we could turn the car around and merge back into traffic. Why were you in the left lane going so fast?" I asked.

"I didn't think I was going fast. When I saw you, I tried to get out of the way and merge into the right lane, but the snow build up between the lanes caused my car to swerve. I lost control of my car and started spinning. That's when I hit you," he explained.

We could both look back at that moment as responsible adults and say, no, we wouldn't do the same thing now, but as a seventeen-year-old girl and a twenty-two-year-old man, and given the same circumstances and naïveté, we would probably do the same thing again.

My mouth was dry from the beer, the cigarettes, and the emotion. We had said all there was to say. We couldn't dissect it any further. While it didn't feel complete and over, it felt like this was all we could do. He walked me back to the lobby and I hugged him again. But this time I wanted to.

I walked back to the hotel room in a fog of emotion. Matthew and Kirk immediately turned off the TV and looked at me with expectant eyes. "It was good," was all I could muster. They came up and their huge arms embraced me. I allowed myself to fold into their love. My brain was full and I could feel the stirrings of a shift in my heart.

A year later, I found myself returning to Victoria for a conference. I called Harvey to see if he was free for dinner.

We met at a restaurant as if we were old friends. This time, I was excited to see him, for he was like a missing link in my life. He and I intimately shared the same tragedy, just from opposite sides. While I shared this experience with my brother and sister, it was from the same side and we each had our own pain to deal with. Harvey and I were the two who made the most intense, life-altering decisions resulting in the loss of my leg. To connect with him again felt like putting in the last piece to a puzzle.

Our evening was sweet. This time we connected; two trampled hearts, picking each other up off the roadway. He talked about the woman he was dating and her children; I talked about my lousy love life. I told him about my herbal studies and my work. He talked passionately about his alter-ego life as a karaoke DJ. We smiled a lot into each other's eyes.

We didn't want the evening to end, but he had to go to a karaoke gig. He walked me back to my hotel. We stood in the lobby holding hands, looking at each other, beaming. Anyone looking at us would have thought we were lovers with a special secret. They would have been half right. We did have a secret. We knew that a lovely dinner, laughing and crying, pulled us out of the sadness and pain we carried all these years because we came to the table with love and acceptance. The evening ended with the sweetest kiss I'll ever have. It was beyond a romantic kiss or a fatherly kiss. It was the kiss of forgiveness.

And he really didn't even need to say he was sorry.

Living Peace

Hagit Ra'anan

The love of a single heart can make a world of difference.
—IMMACULÉE ILIBAGIZA,
Left to Tell

Jewish tradition required that I perform the Jewish *mitzvot*, or commandments, at age twelve. The Bat Mitzvah ceremony signaled my entry into the responsibilities of adulthood. I turned twelve in 1962, when the Old City of Jerusalem was under the rule of the Jordanian kingdom. Jews were forbidden to enter then. A fence separated us from the land that is most sacred and holy to us, but as a Bat Mitzvah gift to me, my father lifted me up and over the fence. Jordanian snipers stood nearby as my father said, "Run . . . touch the outer wall of the Old City . . . and run back. This is your initiation ceremony."

Our family followed Jewish traditions, and I ran as my father told me to run. I also accepted the belief that prevailed in our home: There never would be peace between Arabs and Jews.

This story begins before I was born. In 1923, my grandfather feared the future for Jews in Europe so he took his family out of Lita (Poland at the time) and moved to Israel. My grandmother's sister, Rosa, chose to stay in Europe and she didn't survive the Holocaust. I never met her.

In 1947, my parents became part of Etzel, or Irgun, a right-wing underground movement. My father was chief commander of the Irgun in the Jerusalem district. Terrible things happened during that period, and I often question my father's actions. Still, I love him and I understand that he did what he believed he had to do.

There were few days of peace in my life. At age thirty-two, as a daughter of the Israeli Nation, I had lived through six wars, served in the army, and lost many friends in those wars. The most devastating loss for me occurred in the Lebanon War in 1982. During the first week near Beirut, a Palestinian killed Haim, my beloved partner for life. When he died, I was five months pregnant with our first child, but I soon miscarried. I believe the precious embryo left me to travel with his father, my beloved, whose very name means "life" in Hebrew, on his journey home. I was alone with a broken heart.

Deep depression overwhelmed me. Why go on? I couldn't answer that question, but after four years, I realized that I didn't want to live as a victim, and I began to look for the gift in the pain of losing my beloved and our child. There were many reasons for feeling anger, loss, guilt, and fear, but I chose to take responsibility and to create circumstances in which I could grow. I began to realize there is a hidden gift in even the most difficult situation. I understood that negative emotions were not serving me, that I needed purpose in my life. Gradually, an inner peace emerged out of depression as I acknowledged that I could only change myself. I couldn't change the world or anyone else, but I could change myself and let good radiate from me. Good or bad, we create what we are.

I began to practice meditation and healing, first for myself and then, after the assassination of Prime Minister Rabin, for others. Healing is for individuals, and it also is for nations. I believe in its power because I have seen it work.

To promote healing between Israel and Palestine—the nations and the citizens—I began to work with Palestinian children, hoping to change their perceptions of Israelis. The names of those children may appear to be mere drops in a vast ocean, but for me, each name has shape and heart and soul. When I say the name, I see the child.

The Intifada, the Palestinian uprising against Israel, was mounted to end the Israeli occupation of Palestinian lands. In the seemingly never-ending conflict, that occupation, of course, had been the Israeli response to Palestinian attacks in the early 1990s. Atef had been grievously injured during the Intifada. He was completely paralyzed except for some slight movement in his right hand. It was the horrific result of trying to save his brother, who was killed in the Jabalya refugee camp where they lived.

There was no help at all for Atef in Palestine. He wanted to enroll in the university, an impossible goal without a wheelchair. I appealed to a generous individual for help, and an electric wheelchair was obtained for half price. Atef went on to attend university.

Allah, a child from a small Palestinian village near Hebron, played a "game" during the first days of the Intifada. The game was throwing stones at Israeli soldiers. After a rubber bullet hit him in the eye, there was no proper treatment and both of his eyes became infected. He was at risk of losing his sight. Others helped me, and we were able to get him to an Israeli hospital where the doctor advised sending him to England for an operation. Through a series of miracles, Allah was sent to England, and after two months, he telephoned, saying, "Grandma, I want you to know that I can ride my bicycle." What wonderful news!

When little Allah was happy about clothes and sweets that I gave him (especially the sweets), he asked his mother, "Yama, is she Jewish? Are you sure she is Israeli?" That broke my heart, and the message was clear: There is so much healing yet to be completed. How very difficult it is to see beyond the limits we ourselves set.

Someone told Barah to climb onto an electrical pylon and hoist the Palestinian flag on it. He did what he was told and lost both of his arms and legs from the powerful electrical shock. Spirit guided me to the financial resources that we needed, and we were able to take Barah to Chicago for surgery and prosthetic legs and arms.

A friend gave me a wonderful gift for my fiftieth birthday. At Wolfson Medical Center, near Tel Aviv, a doctor had made it known that he was willing to perform open-heart surgery on Palestinian children in need. At a reception to raise funds for the hospital, my friend bought my gift, one heart operation. As a result of her generosity, a three-year-old child from the Askar camp had the lifesaving surgery on my birthday.

For me, these children are not just drops in a vast ocean.

Before the Intifada, it was my practice to take Israelis to the Gaza Strip for weekend visits. I wanted them to see the Palestinians' beautiful achievements: new neighborhoods, roads, airport, and cultural and rehabilitation centers. Because I believe there is a chance that fear will dissolve when people know each other, I also took them to the refugee camps where Israelis and Palestinians could meet. Fear is the real enemy.

The second Intifada started in October of 2000, but it was still possible to obtain hospitalization and health care in Israel's hospitals for the Palestinians. It was my practice to visit the injured Palestinians in hospitals. Bringing them clothes, food and medicine were the small things available to ease their suffering. This also gave us a chance to get to know each other, and realize that there are many of us who are willing to work for peace.

Whenever there is a terror attack on Israel, my pain is doubled. First, I fear for my own people, who will be killed or injured just for being in the "wrong place"—a restaurant, a bus, a disco—at the "wrong time." Then there will be immediate revenge by Israel on the Palestinians, and so I also fear for my other "children." A terror attack on Israel means that the Palestinians will also suffer.

During the war of summer 2006, I spent many of my days with Israeli children, who stayed for weeks in smothering shelters. Did I help them or did they help me? It must be both, but it is so little in such a huge ocean of pain. I am grateful for even the little, which helps my healing. If only I could visit the children in the Gaza strip and those in Lebanon . . . children are children are children.

I spend time with Israeli children in the northern district of Israel—Jews, Muslims, Druze, and Christians . . . it seems the Almighty does not discriminate; all the children suffer in this insane scenario.

Imagine that you are with me when I tell the children about Sadako Sasaki. Sadako was a Japanese girl who was born in Hiroshima during World War II. She was exposed to atomic radiation and the result was a diagnosis of leukemia when she was twelve years old.

Shortly before her death, she made a commitment to fold one thousand paper cranes. She knew about the ancient Japanese legend, which says the one who folds one thousand cranes will be granted a wish.

When I share this story with the children, I tell them that Sadako's wish included them. It was her wish that the children of the world, all children everywhere, would never again be part of conflicts between adults. She wished for children always to be left out of these terrible events.

Then I tell them that Sadako was too sick to complete folding her cranes—but now, they can do it for her. They can fold one thousand paper cranes. You should see the sparkle in their eyes. "Yes!" Enthusiastically and immediately they vow, "We will fold one thousand paper cranes. We will make it happen for all the children of the world."

Think now about those little fingers folding small colored papers into the shape of cranes. See the children as they close their eyes and pray silently for peace on earth, blowing the spirit of their prayers into the paper birds. Hear their wish to spread the message across Mother Earth to all children. Their prayers will echo into eternity.

I tell this story in remembrance of my beloved Haim. Even in death, he and I are one. I am his living gravestone. My entire existence is based on his legacy. He is the core of everything I do.

Shaman in the Streets

Mama Donna Henes

Do the best you can in the place where you are and be kind.

—Scott Nearing,
*Visionaries: The 20th Century's
100 Most Inspirational Leaders*

Years ago, when the planes flew into the Twin Towers, I was out of the country and it took me more than a week to be able to get past the sealed U.S. borders and return home to New York. One thought consumed my mind during that agonizing week of separation from my house, pets, friends, and the city I loved: I craved to be of service to my community, to do whatever healing I could, as I had been doing for so long.

As an urban shaman, it had been my job for nearly thirty years to minister to the spiritual needs of my clients, my circles of ritual celebrants and the general population of the city that I loved. The *New Yorker* had dubbed me "the unofficial commissioner of public spirit of New York City," and I took this designation very seriously.

My honey and I had been staying in an idyllic, isolated riverside cabin on the banks of the St. Lawrence in the sparsely populated wilds of upper Quebec where no one spoke English. We only found out about the World Trade Center when we went to the office of the landlady to pay for another night. Her TV was on and she was crying.

During the next week, our days were spent in the parking lot of the gas station in the nearest town, where the only pay phone was located. Hour after hour, we tried in vain to reach family and friends. All planes were grounded. Even though we wanted desperately to get home, we were stuck where we were. Our only consolation was provided by the patisserie next door to the station, which had the best chocolate croissants we had ever tasted.

Our nights were spent in a clapboard shack surrounded by marshland, next to a river where whales swam by, under a canopy of brilliant stars in the black northern sky. We watched the horrifying images of our city under attack on the CBC, with only our French phrasebooks to help us understand what was happening. The situation in New York City was unfathomable; our immediate circumstances in Quebec were surreal.

I was aghast at the destruction and terror wreaked on my hometown. I mourned deeply for the dead and cried out in empathy for the pain of the living. I grieved that the sacred site of so many of the carefree, communal ceremonies that I had facilitated at the World Trade Center over the years was now a constant reminder that there were three thousand people who were slaughtered there.

My ritual relationship with the World Trade Center was long and rich. For more than two decades, it had served as my own personal and public shrine, an urban Stonehenge for an urban shaman. Tens of thousands of people had participated in the cosmic community rituals that I orchestrated. A great many of them worked upstairs in the offices in the twin buildings. Many more, who were tourists from everywhere in the world, were riding to the top of the towers to get a bird's eye view of the Big Apple.

I wondered with trepidation about the fates of all of the building's staff whose names I never knew, the people who had helped to set up and facilitate those joyful seasonal ceremonies—the guards, the sound guys, the helpers with ladders and brooms, the woman with the key to the ladies' restroom. I prayed that they were all safe. And I prayed for all of the thousands of people in those buildings who had added their soulful energy to our celebrations over the years.

I wondered what happened to all those people

on the observation deck that day—the school groups, the Girl and Boy Scout troops, and the thousands of tourists who visited the towers every day. I wondered and I wept. I blessed them all with sanctity and with solemn intentions that their tragic loss would propel us to build the sort of world where people don't blow each other up. Shall we do this in their names?

These prayers begged for an altar, so I created one right there on the rocks of the St. Lawrence shore. I dragged the landlady's three-foot-tall plaster Madonna that had been standing sentinel in her driveway up to the shoreline to watch over our prayers. She was a goddess of compassion in a world gone mad. I picked wildflowers and put them in my toothbrush glass and I lit my travel candle, which I had been carrying for years in my cosmetic bag and had never used.

And in a spot of honor, I placed a small crystal that I always carried with me in my amulet bag. It was a relic from the last ceremony that I had held at the World Trade Center, ironically called, "Keeping the Fires Burning For Peace: A Summer Solstice Sunrise to Sunset Vigil for Peace on the Planet." I used it to offer thanks for the 53,000 people working in the buildings who had been saved from a fiery death that day, and in loving memory of those two mythic megaliths; of all those innocents who had died; of all who had suffered and are suffering still; of all who had helped; and in the name of all of us who needed to heal.

After what seemed like an eternity in limbo, we were finally able to get ourselves to Montreal and catch a train home. During the ten-hour trip, I consulted my tarot cards and contemplated just how I could be of service once I returned. How could I best help? I was desperate to talk, to listen, to minister to my community. It became clear to me that it was the human face of this tragedy and its resulting extraordinary state of affairs that I should choose to focus on. I did not want to lose track of the myriad emotional and spiritual interconnections that people are capable of making—with each other, with their own best selves, and with the greater universal good of all.

When we arrived at last, we were welcomed by a quieter, kinder, gentler city. A delivery guy was just leaving my building as I arrived home with all my heavy travel bags. When he saw me trying to wrestle them up the stairs, he ran to help me, thank goodness. He wouldn't accept a tip and insisted that he just wanted to help. When I asked him if all his relations were safe, he said that they were all fine, but that he felt terrible because he wanted to do something to help. "You just did," I reminded him. He was extremely pleased with the notion that this, too, was peacemaking.

Thank you.

Now I knew just what I had to do. My response to the terrible tragedy was to undertake a "Walk Your Talk Pilgrimage," to take to the streets and talk to everyone I met. To offer what succor I could. So, first thing the next morning, I hit the pavement running. One by one, I engaged the people whose paths I crossed: friends, the UPS man, the guard at the bank, the waitress at the coffee shop, the washing-machine repairman—the people who actually live, work, and love in New York City. We engaged in amazingly intimate, sweetly profound conversations that inevitably ended in a hug or an extra-firm handshake.

On the way to the coffee shop with three friends my first morning back in Brooklyn, I ran into my neighbor Monifa walking with another woman. We stopped right there in the middle of the street, traffic not withstanding. (And, miraculously, nobody honked.)

"How are you?"

"How are you?"

"No one dead?"

"Everyone OK?"

We ran our eyes up and down each other looking for signs, for clues of damage. Then all six of us embraced in relief and mutual comfort—and then we introduced ourselves to the ones in this circle whom we didn't know. We hugged first and asked names later! It was surely a sign of sanity in psychotic times. (And still, nobody honked.)

Thank you.

I went to visit my local fire precinct, Ladder Company No. 2 (now known as Rescue Squad 1), a little more than a week after the conflagration to pay my respects. There was a chalk list of the missing from this firehouse posted outside with eleven names on it. There had clearly been a twelfth, just recently erased, but I didn't have the heart to ask whether this missing firefighter had been found alive or dead. The neighbors had blanketed the sidewalk up and down the street with offerings of flowers, candles, cakes, tears, and messages—one written on World Trade Center stationery and sent by a man as a thank you for saving his life on that fateful day of reckoning.

I shook the hands of one traumatized, but sturdy, young firefighter and thanked him. I engaged his misting eyes with my own and told him that I prayed that their dedication and sacrifice would be the foundation of a new way to live together as a world community. He locked my eyes in his and squeezed my hand and bit his quivering lip. He had seen quite enough of war.

Thank you.

At the bank, I greeted the lobby guard as usual. I asked him if he was OK. "Not really," he told me as his eyes filled with tears. His stepfather had been in the building. He had escaped, but was shaken to the core. The guard, whom I talk to practically every day and whose name I am ashamed to admit I do not know, said that he felt that his stepdad would never be the same, like some Vietnam vets he has known who will never be the same.

Then, he confessed to me something remarkable. Actually, it was the most profound thing that I have heard anyone, anywhere, say on the subject. "I hate my uncle," he told me. "And I have hated my uncle for so long that now I hate anyone who looks like my uncle. 'Why for you got to go look like my uncle?'" he quoted himself in his West Indian lilt. "Now I have to hate you." He looked me right in the eyes and said that he realized now how wrong that is, that he can no longer hate all uncle look-alikes, and that he is now even working on trying not to hate his uncle.

Thank you.

I called Judith, one of the women who regularly attended my circles, who was feeling particularly despondent. A nurse, she had immediately run to one of the hospitals on Tuesday morning to lend a hand, but after the first batch of the injured passed through the emergency room, there was no one else to help.

An ill wind had blown the smoke, ash, and smoldering bits and pages of paper from the World Trade Center into her yard three miles away on the other side of the Battery Tunnel. She was worried about her two small children. She was desperate to move out of this place of feeling helpless. "I wish there was something that I could do."

"You could call Linda," I suggested, knowing that she'd had a recent, painful falling-out with a good friend of hers. She allowed, as she had known deep down, all along, that in light of everything that had just happened, she should call, she *wanted* to call. But she couldn't. "Just do it, honey. Make peace." And she did! And they did!

Thank you. Thank you. Thank you.

I spent the rest of that September and most of October in the streets of my home borough of Brooklyn, walking and talking to friends, neighbors, and strangers alike. I was touched to the core by every single soul

I met. Like most folks, I have often wondered how I would react in an emergency. Would I panic or would I be able to keep my cool and do what was necessary, what was helpful and healing?

As it turned out, I am pleased to say, I *was* able to rise to this crisis with my head clear and my heart open, ready, willing, and eager to help in whatever way I could. And so did eight million other New Yorkers who responded to the horrifying circumstances with courage, compassion, love, and hope. Most miraculous of all to me was that there was no call for war or retribution from the people of New York. We experienced the horror and destruction of a terrorist attack in our homeland and in our front yard first-hand. And that was quite enough for us, thank you very much. While the president called for war and was cheered nationwide, the families of the victims of the attack were adamant in their objection to inflicting violence on others. "Not in my daughter's name," they proclaimed. "Not in the name of my son, my husband, my friend, my beloved wife."

Thank you so very much.

An intense white light, an inner glow, even now, these many years later, emanates from the people of New York City. We in our beleaguered town have tasted grace. In the hardest of times, we managed to transcend what made us human and grow to embody what makes us humane. I am so proud to have been both a participant in and a witness of this munificence.

But how slippery is the slope from the heights

of compassion and empathy back to blame and resentment! I am not immune to these base emotions, I must admit, nor am I deaf to the call to judgment. I believe in my heart that peace is possible, but it takes such great courage to sustain it every minute of every day. Maintaining peace is often harder than fighting, I find.

When I reflect on the events surrounding 9/11 and its aftermath, I feel challenged to be vigilant, to discover and confront the parts of myself that resist peace and misdirect my feelings of anger and opposition onto others. Like my wise and honest friend the bank guard, I, too, have been harboring a seething, unresolved, unforgiving, and unsatisfactory antagonism toward a close relative for quite some time. My deteriorated relationship with my brother Joseph is the only one in all the six decades of my life that has never been healed. It is the only grudge that I carry. And it is weighing me down.

Yet I have been so reluctant to release that heart-heavy load. Rather than giving up my feelings of having been wronged and moving toward a new détente, based on mutual respect and acceptance, I flood my mind with charming memories from our childhood; memories that may or may not even be accurate after all these years, memories that cause me to re-resent him all over again for not being the way he once was—or the way that I wish he could be. This self-inflicted torture-by-nostalgia does nothing but make me feel bad.

My ire exists in part because he is so intractable and stern in his religious and political views. He is positively messianic in his rigid perception of right and wrong, good and evil, us and them. He knows with certainty who his enemies are and that God is on his side, while I struggle with the confused and conflicted impulses of my emotions toward him. To forgive? To withhold? To embrace? To ignore? I have stubbornly clung to the pain of our antagonism even as I have anguished over my inability to let it go.

And then, while I was immersed in writing this peace piece and revisiting once again all of the inspiring peacemakers that I met on my 9/11 pilgrimage, I experienced a profound "aha!" breakthrough in understanding my private little cold war. I realized that I was condemning Joseph for perpetuating an atmosphere of dissonance, and all the while my condemnation of him was creating the same damning disconnection—a worse one, really, because it was so hypocritical.

I finally understood that if I were unable to forgive him for being so rigid, I would be just like the parts of him that I despised. Though, of course, I knew this all along intellectually, this new knowing was more visceral and deeply resonant. The revelation felt like a punch in the gut, knocking the air right out of me and leaving me miraculously, mercifully empty of rage.

Let there be peace on earth, and let it begin with me.

Thank you.

I finished writing this essay about my pilgrimage late at night and was able to sleep in peace after having finally confronted my demons and enjoyed a shift in consciousness. And don't you know that early the next morning the phone woke me? It was Joseph, calling from Chicago to tell me he would be coming to town soon and that he hoped we could get together.

Thank you!

Promising *Daylilies*

Alice Butler Collins

*To every thing there is a season, and a time to every
    purpose under the heaven:
A time to be born, and a time to die; a time to plant and
    a time to pluck up that which is planted;
A time to kill, and a time to heal. . . .
A time to weep, and a time to laugh; a time to mourn and
    a time to dance. . . .
A time to embrace, and a time to refrain from embracing;
A time to get, and a time to lose; a time to keep, and a
    time to cast away;
A time to rend, and a time to sew; a time to keep silence,
    and a time to speak;
A time to love, and a time to hate; a time of war, and a
    time of peace.*

—Ecclesiastes 3:1–8

It was a Saturday afternoon in late 2001. I was seated in a crowded meeting room with young, middle-aged and silver-haired women and men from every part of the Chicago urban metropolis. The workshop brochure promised that participants would be allowed the opportunity to have a life-changing experience. Everyone in the room had questions: "How?" "What if?" "Do you think I can?" Everyone was searching for answers. Some seemed happy, some angry and fearful. During the session, there were intense discussions about a wide range of topics. I watched and waited. I waited and watched. The air in the room was hot and dry. I shifted from right to left in a steel folding chair that somehow managed to get smaller and harder the longer I sat. Both sides of the chair were hard and flat. As I looked around the room, only a few things came to my mind: *Should I stop payment on the $300.00 check I wrote for these workshops? Can I get iced café mocha nearby? Maybe I should find the closest ladies' room and hide out for a while.* The logical side of my mind slowly took control and I knew that the only way to get my money's worth was to pay attention and to put forth more effort. I straightened my back, placed my feet on the floor and forced myself to stay on task.

Earlier in the year, I had made a sudden decision to retire from my job, ending a thirty-seven-year career in education. Friends, family, and co-workers gave me a huge celebration. I was overwhelmed by cards, gifts, and the flashing bulbs of cameras. The change in my lifestyle was rapid, but the adjustment period was slow.

Months later, a friend had said, "After I retired, I went to a series of workshops that helped me make the transition. You might find the process useful." I took my friend's advice and signed up for a three-day workshop. When I thought about my future, I knew I wanted to read, think, travel, and _____. Somehow, I could never finish the sentence, never fill in that blank.

Now in the workshop, the presenter said, "Your next task is to think of a promise you made to someone important in your life. A promise you made, but for some reason, you didn't keep. Write a letter to the person that explains what you're going to do about your broken promise."

I hastily searched my memory, struggling to find something I could write about. Finally, I thought about my friend Mary Ann and a promise I made to her about three weeks before she died. I was tempted to ask if it was okay to write to a person who was dead. Before I could, my pen started to move slowly across my yellow legal pad. Ten minutes later, when the workshop leader asked the participants if anyone wanted to share a letter, I stood up and headed to the microphone. For the first time in two days, I started to honestly speak to the seventy people in the room:

> Hi, Mary Ann,
>
> It's been a long time since we were able to talk. But I think about you when I am

reading a good book and want to discuss what it really means, or when I'm shopping for a new dress and want to know how I really look, or when I have to weigh the pros and cons before I make a really difficult decision. I'm writing this letter because I have some good news and some bad news. You probably already know, but I need to tell you for myself. Good news first: I know you remember when we worked on our ten-year career goals. Over the years, I worked hard to achieve my goals. When I reached a goal, I always picked up the phone to talk to you, but for the past six years, I couldn't reach you where you are now. I remember when we worked as partners in a high school support program, you said, "We need time to dream. Let's cut our lunch hour short each day and get back to work fifteen minutes early. Then on Friday, we can have a whole hour to discuss dreams and plans."

Many of those dreams became my career and life goals. Before I retired, I became the principal of the school where we met and wrote our goals. As principal, I remembered the goals we had shared to improve conditions for the school and the community. I took out that list of goals and I had a blueprint for success. You always said, "The plan works if you work it." As usual, you were right.

Bad news. I remember our last conversation and the promise I made. Somehow, I forgot the promise until about ten minutes ago. Maybe I really blocked that conversation from my mind. But now I recall that it was the morning before you left on a hospital plane headed for Nebraska. We were sitting at your kitchen table when you said, "There is one more thing that I want you to do after I'm gone. Promise me that you will write a story about the last few months of my life."

I said, "Why?"

"We've both learned valuable life lessons during the last sixteen months of my illness."

"That's true, but why write about it?"

"Because somewhere there are two friends who are wondering if they can face an uncertain future and remain friends."

"Yes," I said. "We did it and we both grew in different ways."

"Share our experiences," you said.

"How?" I asked.

"Tell the truth."

"There's one problem. I can't write."

"You can write this story," you said with confidence. "You're the only person who can."

"I'll try," I said.

"That's not good enough," you scolded. "Do a good job or my spirit will come back and nag you. Growing up, my mother told me Irish ghost stories, so I know exactly what to do when I'm in the spirit world. I'll always be around. Trust me. It's in my DNA."

"You've always been persistent," I said. "No, actually, you're just plain stubborn."

We both laughed until tears were rolling down our cheeks. When we could talk again, we bent over a pad of paper and outlined a book. But I didn't keep my promise. I don't know why, so I'm not going to give you any excuses. Now I'm ready to get started. I feel better just writing this letter. I know that you are going to love the story. I think I'm going to call it Daylilies. *Did I say I miss you? 'Cause I really do. I know that you will forgive me because you always understood me. Well, so long for now. (I never learned how to say goodbye.) Thanks so much for just being you.*

Your friend throughout eternity,
Alice

When I finished reading the letter, there were people in the room who had tears in their eyes. Others said, "Thanks for reminding me about the power of true friendship." In less than fifteen minutes, I had taken a leap of faith.

As the workshop continued, I was actively involved. I made a plan. I started taking writing workshops. I joined two writing groups. I bought a new computer and a tape recorder, and organized a home office. I learned about the power of both the written and the spoken word. Slowly, I removed the blocks that kept me from writing and grieved the loss of my best friend. Sharing my writing with strangers was different and sometimes hard. But the spirit kept affirming that I was on the right path.

For years, my friend Mary Ann enjoyed starting her day with a cup of coffee as she looked out the window at her garden. Her garden was filled with wild flowers that reminded her of her childhood home in rural Nebraska. I have never been a gardener, but she insisted that I take daylilies from her garden and plant them outside my kitchen window. Mary Ann told me that daylilies are perennials and if you plant them where they'll get plenty of morning sunlight, give them space to get bigger, prune the dead leaves, and water the plants, they will grow. I followed her advice and my daylilies bloom when the season changes to this day.

Mary Ann loved her flowers and I am just now starting to understand why. Every spring, my daylilies create a stunning display of unending color. The ruffled blooms blend together into a rainbow of lavender, crimson, orange, garnet, and pearl. In a profusion of color, the blooms explode in the sunlight, bursting as they reach toward the sky and celebrate the day. The blooms scream: "Look at me now, don't take me for granted—take a minute. Right now." Each bloom lasts for only one day—twenty-four hours—but the plant will produce new blooms each day and continues to return year after year.

Since the workshop years ago, I have learned how to write. I have shared Mary Ann's life lessons in poetry, performance, stories, and articles. During the 2009 concert of the Chicago affiliate of the National Association of Black Storytellers, I told a story based on the "girlfriend dialogues" that Mary Ann and I used to have. After the event, one woman said, "Thank you for telling the story. I know now that I can help my friend." Another woman said, "You're telling my story."

I grew when I found the courage to trust God and let the spirit guide me. I worked through my grief and kept my last promise to my spiritual sister. This friend came into my life for only a season, but she somehow keeps me blooming year after year.

TWO

Creating My Destiny

We shape our self
to fit this world

and by the world
are shaped again.

The visible
and the invisible

working together
in common cause,

to produce
the miraculous.

—DAVID WHYTE,
"Working Together"

We were born to manifest the glory of God that is within us. It's not just in some of us; it's in everyone.
—MARIANNE WILLIAMSON,
A Return to Love

In this chapter, each woman tells us a true story about responding to her own inner call. Each shares with us how she found her pathway to her unique destiny. Like these women, all of us participate in the creation of our destinies. The wisdom of Rumi's words lets us know we are prepared for new thresholds:

"Everything you want and need is already inside you."

Heed your desires. Listen to the longings that haunt your nights. They are quiet calls to follow your soul's wild heartbeat. Spirit has graced us with light for our journeys, and even the adversity that sometimes threatens a detour from our envisioned paths is a worthy guide. The truth of a Navajo saying tells us to bless our challenges for they are big teachers for us and can lead us home to our true essential natures.

Creation and destiny help make the music of these stories. Connection to creation and the creator gives these women a sense of purpose as they express themselves in rare ways. The love of creator naturally carries some to move their bodies to experience the divine, follow their dreams, forgive when betrayed, and to never give up in times of anguish. Each of these women responded to a unique call to do something that seemed impossible or unusual to others. In their stories, they share with us a critical moment that both challenged and fulfilled them.

No woman's life is too small to make a difference in the world. Anita Roddick puts it in perspective: "If you think your life is too small to have impact, try sleeping with a mosquito."

Telling the Bees

S. Kelley Harrell

Live the questions now. Perhaps then, someday far in the future, you will gradually, without ever noticing it, live your way into the answer.

—RANIER MARIA RILKE,
Letters to a Young Poet

Central to many ancient shamanic traditions are honeybees, the conductors of souls to the afterlife and keepers of sacred knowledge. So it was that there arose in folklore the custom of "telling the bees," or letting them know when a loved one had passed on in order that they could fly the dear soul on careful wings to Source. To those who thought the bees were themselves the soul of the loved one, meaningful discourse with the bees enabled peaceful departure. Such was the impact of the sacred honeybee that heaving up the hive became a tradition in early cultures, lifting up the coffin at the same time as the hive was lifted, thus beginning the loved one's procession to the Beyond.

As a child, I had a more practical experience with bees. My grandfather was a beekeeper, which I realized at a young age was part hobby, part meditation, and part religion for him. I spent long hours watching his smoke-shrouded form move with hypnotic grace, gently lifting dripping frames to scrape clean, then refill with light, fresh comb. Then there would be sticky trails throughout the kitchen with the dining room table moved out to make room for the extractor, hives stacked to the ceiling. He never let me touch the fragrant sheets of wax cells, which were too delicate for my undiscerning hands. Instead, my sister and I were allowed to hammer new frames together while he spun comb and tales—never-ending allegories depicting how poorly most human strategies for success measured against the finesse and poise in the culture of a hive.

The work was hard, but we were always rewarded with as much honey, butter and bread as our tingling teeth could stand. He did have a knack for always bringing about the sweetness of situations, though that perhaps wasn't always his intention. Extracting season meant long afternoons laced with lessons about the efficiency of the drones in getting the housework done, or about the hierarchy of the hive ensuring that authority was respected and never questioned, all to maintain the integrity of the whole. I respected my grandfather, maybe more than anyone in my life, though I did wonder how he could infer such complex life lessons from mute insects.

One summer late in my sixteenth year, I heard bees *talking*. Mid-afternoon on a Saturday in early June, there was a persistent thrumming just outside our kitchen window. My grandfather went out to investigate while my mom, great aunt, and I prepared supper. He returned to report a rare find—a swarm had settled into an old hollow table base in our backyard. It wasn't a common thing to find honeybees taking up residence in random places, particularly when their immaculate white hives dotted our property. Even more odd than the rogue hive, he reported, two virgin queen bees were sharing the ill-suited colony.

Multiple queens in a hive could be a precursor to disaster. From what my grandfather had taught me, I knew that they wouldn't likely tolerate each other's presence, and the social and work organization of their hive could suffer for it. My grandfather would have to move the swarm from its bizarre location into a proper hive, and to maintain balance, he would need to separate the two queens. Bees want stability in their hive, and they will work to great lengths to defuse any confusion of roles. One queen and her drones simply had to go.

Diligently, he worked the rest of the afternoon

and into early evening to give each queen her own space. I could tell he was thrilled to experience such a natural gift, as the only time he spoke was when spoken to. The adults in the family weren't as accustomed as I was to his work with bees, and naturally they had lots of questions, all of which he patiently entertained. I could tell he wasn't used to having an audience to his interaction with the bees. All things considered, he was exceptionally quiet. My mother, stepfather, and great-aunt and uncle all peered at him out the window *oohing* and *ahhing* between samples from pots on the stove, watching as his puffs of smoke settled the piping queens. Unflapped as I was by the whole affair, even I poked my head out to observe him. I felt particularly special watching him perform a ritual with the bees that he, himself, had never experienced. It was a remarkable moment, and I marveled at how lovingly he worked in the sweltry heat swathed under the heavy veil and gear. The image of him working was recorded in my mind.

I don't know exactly what transpired for my grandfather as he brought balance to the colony and created spaces for new growth and life. He had kept bees most of his adult life but, at seventy-one, he encountered his first occurrence of multiple virgin queens and the excitement of moving them. The act of relocating the swarm was intense enough on its own—altering the culture of the bees, enabling new organization elsewhere. The procedure also was very much alive with the baser human conflict of making the wild tame. Where these virgin queens had come from, their purposes for colliding in the wild hive—those were mysteries. I was sure that these things had been foremost in my grandfather's mind, too, though he did not say them aloud.

What I knew from the moment he finally sat down to our late supper was that something in him had changed. My grandfather was quiet, troubled even, and he departed early for bed.

As unique a weekend as it had been, I chalked the strange events up to the whims of Nature, though a distinct heaviness settled over our home in the days after. Everyone else seemed to carry on as normal, but around every corner, the ambiance of our home was oppressive to me. I couldn't name it, nor did I speak of it to anyone. And though I knew the muzziness I felt around me had something to do with those elusive queens, I did not approach my grandfather about my feelings. What was I going to say? "Pappy, whatever blew those bees into our backyard drafted something awful into my heart." Neither my experience nor my belief system could conceive or sustain a correlation of the events of Nature with a change in the dynamic of my family—a shift in my life. My grandfather's people were part Cherokee, and although he respected their traditions in his relationship to the earth and he passed that honor on to me, his demeanor was such that his old-fashioned sensibilities would not have entertained such a capricious emotional expression from me. I kept my foreboding to myself.

That next week my great aunt died. She had been very sick for quite a long while and, for the first time in my young life, I experienced the paradox of merciful death. The loss of her was a significant one to us all, as she was our family matriarch. She was the cook, the hostess, the comforter, and the keeper of all the mysterious secrets for how to do just about everything. Her loss was particularly difficult for my great uncle and my grandfather, as they had all hailed into adulthood together. They were bonded by decades of laughter, loss, war, and children. At her death, I felt compelled to carry out many of the tasks that she would have done for us—making sure everyone else was fed, comfortable, rested. I turned seventeen amid grief and great confusion in our family.

A month after her death, my grandfather and I stood at the point where his yard sloped into mine. The shortened days and browned grass signaled the time of year to move the hives in the western part of the state— at our ancestral family home in the Smokies—and he would be leaving home for a while. His tone was un- characteristically severe as he rather harshly shook my shoulders and told me to watch his garden, specifically the tomatoes, while he was gone. They would be ripe any day and he did not want the many rows of them to go to waste. He was gentle by nature and rarely, if ever, had he laid a hand on me. I was dumbstruck. The cicadas scratched a song together, and his eyes shone and my being went silent. Without understand- ing how, I knew he wasn't just going to tend his hives in the mountains. He was going to the bees to finish something, and he was leaving me with the impeccable understanding that I was to take on his duties in his absence. I felt this truth deep in my soul, along with an unimaginable sadness. I stood there feeling foolish as tears streamed down my face, nodding while he barked instructions to me that I did not hear. He patted my back gently as he wiped at his own eyes, then turned to head back to his house. I remained rooted in place, stunned. Crickets chirped and fireflies flickered in the nearby dogwood. Mosquitoes hung in clouds in the balmy twilight air as if it were any other July evening. I stood between our yards and cried, knowing something cosmic had transpired between us, but not knowing for the life of me what it was.

My grandfather did not come back from the mountains. He died exactly a month to the day after my great aunt. I spent the rest of the summer numb, watching honey ooze down two newly painted hives, tomatoes rotting in the garden.

Typically, shaman are chosen in one of three ways: they are spontaneously called, they elect to become such, or they inherit the role. I would like to say that I was furtively called, and that with the aid of stellar emissaries, I put these poignant happenings together on the spot. That from them, I learned to turn sacred messages culled from the world around me into useful guidance for my life. I'd like to report that I quickly and happily chose my path, with an epiphany springing from information I read later that summer

in a local journal. In a feature story, a woman chron-
icled her work with a Native American shaman. That
was the first time I'd heard the word. I anticipated the
shaman's actions and intentions more quickly than I
could read the paragraphs. Ten years later, after I had
devoted solitary study to shamanism after going to a
shaman for healing, I'd like to report that I realized
my life experiences had been whispering to me what
my role in shamanic work would be. But the truth is,
I did not.

Instead, my spirit teachers set me on a course of
personal tribulation and adventure that would prove
to me over and over that I am one who walks between
realms to the betterment of her tribe. It is now twenty
years since that summer. My growth into the role of
shaman occurred later in my adulthood. The insight
from my growth has shown me it was that summer
that I first truly owned that my experiences were different from most. There were nervous times during my
childhood when I awakened at night with the dead in
my bedroom, or seeing in broad daylight that more
than the living walked the halls of my house. I felt I
was the shaky axis between worlds when I watched my
grandfather move those prophetic queens. At the time,
I did not know what the feelings were. I only knew
that the presence of the queens was significant, that
watching him move them stirred deep emotions, and
that the deaths of my family's elders somehow created
me as an unwilling ancestor to myself.

North America, a land of diverse spiritual tradition, lacks a formal nod to the role of shaman at its heart. My own traditional education was lacking, but I sought and created the instruction and initiation that I needed. Despite rather unorthodox learning and teaching, I thought perhaps my abilities as a shaman were a fluke, that some past-life cell was finally dominant in the current matrix; that odd coincidences over a summer of my life foretold an equally bizarre life path. The truth may actually be a great deal closer to home than I knew.

Perhaps my affinity to the unseen was inherited. It may be that my grandfather heard the voices of the bees far beyond the earthly construct of the hive but, like me, he had no one to share it with. He had no context for those experiences or the information he gained from them. Maybe his ability to commune with the spirits of Nature was so ingrained that it didn't need to be spoken; maybe it was as commonplace as breathing to him. Or, perhaps he was not consciously aware of it at all, but moved through his life in a state of grace for others to observe and marvel at his ease in communicating with Grandmother Earth's creatures.

To this day, I don't know what the bees told my grandfather, or maybe what he told them. I do not feel it my place to ask. But if I had to guess, I would say it was something about knowing that the timing was right for his and my aunt's transition, and that with the bees' care, he could relax into the changes coming into his life force. I would say that the bees assured him that despite the sweeping loss of a full generation, my family would create the way to graduate into its next role of maturity. And I'm fairly certain that they would have mentioned to my grandfather that I needed special care for a shift into my own awareness. They would have affirmed that the time he spent with me in his life and the legacy he would pass to me as he began his death-walk had fully fostered my ability to consciously, soulfully, intentionally become *me*.

I know, too, that if he did say anything at all to those queens, it would have been simply a resounding, "Yes!"

I Caught Sight of Angels

Suni Paz

It is love that reveals to us the eternal is us and in our neighbors.

—MIGUEL DE UNAMUNO,
Tragic Sense of Life

When my first son, Juan Cruz, was about a year old, my husband Carlos and I moved to the province of Entre Ríos (which means "between rivers") in northeastern Argentina. We were absolutely broke and jobless, but ready to take life by the horns. A relative had invited us to be overseers at his ranch "with no comforts to speak of," as he put it, but rent-free. We were young and desperate, with a baby to feed and dreams of embarking on an Angora rabbit farm venture, so we felt compelled to accept.

Paraná was the nearest city to the farm. We could reach it by boat and the ride up the Paraná River was idyllic. At that time of the year, the trees alongside its banks were covered with resplendent little lilac-colored flowers. Their foliage gave a sweet, soft scent. The moon was full, and we wanted to think that it was smiling over our dreams. From the lower deck, the sound of harps playing *guarañas*, the romantic songs of the area, accompanied the movement of the water. The music softened the sting of our anxieties.

A bus picked us up from the city and brought us five country blocks to our new dwelling. The rectangular house seemed adequate. It had three big rooms and a kitchen, with a large back room for our first rabbits.

The first surprise was that there was no electricity. We would have to get up at dawn and go to bed at dusk. The bathroom had only half-completed plumbing. No showers or baths were to be found. We understood that, in the traditional farm style, we would have to take turns bathing in a wooden tub. The water was unsafe to drink. One could see little moving critters in it. To drink it, we would have to boil it and pass it through a colander made of a suede-like material. The cooking stove looked scary. It was rectangular with a big mouth blackened by many old fires. It had to be lit with coals or wooden logs; a stack of logs was neatly piled up at its sides. I was a bit taken aback by all I would have to do and learn. I barely knew how to cook in a regular kitchen, let alone in this medieval monstrosity. In the days that followed, the outside patio covered with vines was to be my consolation. It had a patch of citrus trees and under them, I spent many siestas, eating from a bowl of oranges, tangerines, and grapefruits while listening to the relentless chitchat of the birds. The day after our arrival, we began cleaning and tilling a patch of land to feed ourselves. We discovered an old horse and a cart that looked like an inheritance from the French Revolution. It became our means of transportation. At times, the horse doubled as an ox, helping us plow the earth.

The generosity of our only neighbor, a skillful old farmer whom we got to know quite well, saved us from starvation. He was moved by our determination to painstakingly learn the skills he knew so well from childhood. He casually left sacks of potatoes, carrots, beets, and cabbages at our doorstep, and he offered us tip after tip on how to enhance our farming skills. He literally sustained us until we got our first vegetables and successfully sold our first packages of Angora hair. By then, our rabbits were reproducing faster than my husband could build new cages to house them. It was an exhausting job. I learned how to give ear and nose drops to each rabbit daily to diminish their tendency to catch colds. A cold could wipe out a generation of rabbits in a matter of hours. I also learned to cut their delicate strands of white hair with sharp scissors and separate it into bundles according to its quality. My haircuts left the rabbits looking like starving little rats with long ears. Without hair, their size was reduced by half, and their pink little bodies gave them a most miserable and helpless look.

Half a year into this work, in the middle of a very cold winter, I fell sick with a violent fever. A bout of hepatitis brought on by contaminated water sent me into quarantine and isolation. Sometimes I lost consciousness. Later, I vaguely remembered having my baby taken away from me, and I was prohibited from handling him.

My husband took over my chores. He began washing the daily diapers of the baby, boiling water in a newly acquired modern stove, cooking, tending the rabbits, feeding the horse and, on top of it, taking care of a helpless, unrecognizable me.

When he began despairing of his ability to survive this inhuman regimen, a complete stranger appeared at our doorstep. She timidly introduced herself: "My name is Teresa." She told my bewildered husband that from then on, she was going to take care of the baby and me. Teresa explained that through the grapevine (the country's most reliable radio), she had heard of our distress. "A young wife was very ill. The husband alone could not cope with all the work, particularly the care of the baby, so here I am."

She lived four miles away with her sister-in-law, Margarita. She helped Margarita raise her five children and kept her company while Margarita's husband traveled in his truck throughout the province digging water holes and constructing windmills. Since the family was left with no means of transportation, she was used to walking.

From the time we arrived at Entre Ríos until then, we had not heard a word from our families. We could not count on them, so my husband gratefully and wholeheartedly accepted Teresa's generous offer of help. For the next four months, Teresa washed my first son's daily diapers in the outdoor basin along with my sheets and my husband's working clothes. She bathed me and my baby, cooked, and fed all of us.

The outside shed was open to the elements and washing there was in itself a merciless chore. Teresa would arrive at dawn and leave at sundown. Efficient and silent, she worked relentlessly throughout the day. I never heard my son crying, so I had no worries. Teresa appeared unfazed by the weather. It didn't matter if it was raining torrentially, lightning crisscrossing the skies, or if the wind seemed to want to erase us from the face of the earth; Carlos could trust that Teresa would be there.

When I slowly regained consciousness and strength, I became aware of her presence. She began bringing my baby to my bedroom door. My Juan Cruz would always be smiling and chirping like a bird. I saw he was well cared for. His cheeks were like two little red apples and his eyes shone with merriment. I also became aware of my clean, ironed sheets, immaculate nightgowns, and the healthy food Teresa would cook especially for me to speed my recovery.

I learned that she was in her forties, had never married, and had been her sister-in-law's midwife.

Her weather-beaten skin made her look much older. Her eyes were soft, but guarded. She was considerably taller than Carlos. One could tell she was used to a life of hard work and sacrifices. She had a great dignity about her that commanded respect. My child was wild about her. She had also gained our hearts. We were profoundly grateful for all she had done for us.

With Teresa's help, I began getting up and about, moving slowly until I acquired enough strength to be able to start helping, and then finally cooking and cleaning by myself. When that day arrived, as quietly and unobtrusively as she came, Teresa left after refusing any payment. She came to help us because we needed it, not for pay, she firmly stated. With our deepest thanks, we let her go.

A few weeks later, we invited Teresa, Margarita, her husband Andrés who had just arrived from one of his trips, and their five kids for *mate* tea, pies, and homemade biscuits. We spent a lovely afternoon under the trees and Margarita taught me how to make bread in an outside oven.

After another visit, Teresa invited us to their home to share a barbecued lamb. They lived with few comforts, but plenty of love in a humble adobe house built by Andrés. In a bare room, around a long rectangular table, Margarita's family and my own sat together to celebrate Andrés's safe return and my recovery. The dinner was to be memorable.

In the center of the table was a well-roasted lamb and a round loaf of bread made by Margarita's hands. There was only one fork and knife to be shared by all and no dishes. Andrés said a prayer of thanks, cut a piece of lamb, took it to his mouth and passed the fork and knife to the next person. Teresa helped the children. As in a ritual, the fork and knife went from hand to hand, making the round several times until the meal ended followed by *mate* tea and home-made cookies. We didn't know it then, but it was going to be the last supper we would ever eat together.

Soon after, Andrés's life changed. He was called to fill a job in another province quite far away, and since it required a long-term commitment, he took his whole family with him. We lost track of one another when my husband and I also had to leave for another country, Chile.

We never saw each other again. At the time, I had not realized it, but I later became aware that without Margarita's consent, Teresa would never have come to us. While Teresa helped us, Margarita was on her own with her five children. So it was by mutual agreement that Teresa had come to our rescue. Their selfless generosity was to be an unforgettable lesson to Carlos and me: Those who had the least were the ones who gave the most of themselves and generously shared with us the little they had.

May this belated story be an act of thanks to them, and a tribute to their memory as well as to the memory of my late husband.

Shadows and Sunshine

Dr. Gladys McGarey

Never give up
No matter what is going on
Never give up. . . .

—"Never Give Up,"
a message given by His Holiness the Dalai Lama
to Ron Whitehead

nd give us grace to endure the dark times. A deep, dark shadow fell over my path on a hot Arizona afternoon. How unkind it is that the worst events sometimes occur in the best of times and the most familiar places!

The time was the forty-sixth year of the marriage of William and Gladys McGarey. We had formed a union, which, if not perfect, was very nearly so in my eyes. Together, we had completed medical school, survived wartime, brought up our children, and established a successful medical practice.

The place was our home, specifically our huge couch, which had always been the secure and friendly center of our family. We had nursed sick children and visited with friends there. Childish voices had told us their wondrous discoveries; adolescents had brought us their wounds to bind up. There we had enjoyed sweet, private moments of marriage. And there it all ended!

Bill had gone to a weekend retreat alone, saying only that he needed time to sort some things out. Solitude apparently met his needs, allowed him to come to grips with his life and compose a letter to me. When he arrived home, we sat together on the couch. He read his letter aloud. He wanted a divorce.

In an instant, I understood why we speak of a broken heart. One's heart does indeed threaten to break. Not only did his words devastate me emotionally and spiritually, the physical pain over my heart was so severe that I had trouble catching my breath. My vision of an ordered future together, with the promise of good years ahead, had vanished with his words.

In my contentment with our relationship and our life, I had been blind. Even when others had questioned his relationship with his nurse, I mentioned it to him only jokingly, and I believed his denials. Even as he asked for a divorce, his denial continued. "Peggy is not the issue," he said.

How did my path bring me to this heartbreak? A rich, full, and busy life began for me in the bleak Himalayan Mountains and in steamy jungles where my parents served as medical missionaries for the Presbyterian Church. My playmates were the Hindu and Muslim children in the villages where they practiced medicine. My aspirations to become a physician began with my kinship with the children and with witnessing my parents' kind and loving care of the ill and injured in those remote places. By the time I was two years old, I knew with certainty that I would be a doctor.

I knew that I had special work to do and that I had been blessed with the talents to do that work. The flame of a candle is a metaphor for my life as a physician. My candle shines with a clear, pure light, but I must be vigilant lest its light become cloudy.

As my father and mother performed surgeries and treated a steady stream of patients, they both chatted pleasantly in the native language, making those who suffered more comfortable and less fearful. When their pains and anxieties were relieved, I saw hope come back into the patients' eyes. As a little child, I applied dressings and made invalids and old people a little more comfortable, and as I tended people who were suffering, my calling was crystal clear.

One day, a first-grade classmate mocked my ambitions: "You can't be a doctor," she said. "Men are doctors. When you grow up, you'll just be a woman, and women are nurses." Those words provoked my first experience with real anger. Even though I understood that she didn't know about my doctor mother or my Aunt Belle, the only physician at a nearby leper's colony, I was as furious as a child can be and shunned my little friend for a long while. When we began to play together again, I settled the dispute by telling her, "I *am* going to be a doctor. You be a nurse if you want to."

When school recessed in November, we left the Himalayas and went to the plains in United Provinces. We traveled from village to village, stayed a week or so in each place, then packed our belongings and medical equipment in an oxcart and moved on to another place of need. Sometimes, we camped beside the Ganges, and I swam in the waters of India's sacred river, making sure to look out for snakes and crocodiles. Since I spoke the language and could roam freely through the villages, I knew the people, and even my child's eyes could see their desperate needs. Even though we sometimes had barely enough food, my parents never reproached me if I brought a hungry child to our table. The child, of course, was always one of the Untouchables. (Because the higher-caste Indians considered missionaries untouchable and forbade their children to eat food contaminated by our touch.) That experience served me well, as it taught me that prejudice is self-limiting and unreasonable.

My parents often saw as many as two hundred patients a day, treating whatever ailment presented, because they were the entire medical community.

There were no emergency rooms, no trauma centers, and no one with whom to consult. It was very simple. If they did not treat, the patients would not be treated. I never saw them turn anyone away. One of my favorite memories illustrates the reach of their service. An elephant driver, a mahout, appeared with a lame elephant. The poor animal was groaning and moaning with each painful step. My father was away, so it fell to my mother to deal with the unexpected patient. She approached the elephant slowly and calmly, but when she probed the wound, he reared and loudly trumpeted his protest. She spoke quietly to him and began to syringe the ulceration with a solution of potassium permanganate. The procedure was painful, and the very large animal threatened by thumping the ground. Mother stood firm, talking to him, occasionally looking him in the eye and patting his leg gently. His threats ceased, and he stood, flinching, as she finished what she needed to do. Over the next days, she continued to flush the wound. As it gradually healed and the pain diminished, the elephant's devotion to my mother grew boundlessly. He followed her wherever she went and often encircled her waist with his trunk, sometimes at the most inconvenient times. She, however, always graciously acceded to his embraces. A gentle giant was thanking the woman who had healed him.

My father taught me to be brave and hardy, often saying, "A faint heart never won anything." That was a lesson that would serve me well when it was time to return to the United States. Gaining entry into and financing medical school was difficult. So was the strangeness of modern life for a young woman who had grown up in primitive conditions. Being alone was difficult. I sorely missed my family.

In 1943, I met William A. McGarey. We fell in love and married. The years that followed were re-markable. We completed medical school and began a family medicine practice. We also began a family and had four children in as many years.

The Korean War put our lives, and those of many other American families, on hold for two years. Left alone to care for our small children, I was also responsible for maintaining our medical office and hospital practices, and attending home births. There were some very hard times, but those were good years nonetheless. I was blessed with my adored children, and I was doing the work I felt I had come into the world to do.

When the Air Force discharged Bill in 1955, we moved to Phoenix, where the Arizona desert appealed to both of us. We practiced medicine side by side. We established a clinic. We helped found the American Holistic Medical Association. We delved into the Edgar Cayce medical literature, pioneered acupuncture in the United States, helped to advance the concept of nutri-tion in medicine, and worked to understand dreams and the connection between spirituality and healing. We authored books, lectured as a team, and completed our family. Throughout those years, we never forgot that a loving, creative home for our six children was our most important task.

Divorce. This alien word entered my life unbidden and unwelcome. Ironically, Bill and I had co-authored a book about marriage. In it, we had said, "As long as we have one arm around each other, the other arm is free to help our fellow humans." Somehow we must have neglected the arm around each other, because we had allowed another person to slip in between us.

That night, I walked with my dog in the desert. I wore Bill's shoes because I had been told that walking in another's shoes enables you to understand what that other person is thinking and feeling. It didn't work that way for me and it didn't help.

But my family did help. The support of my children sustained me even in the worst moments. Friends were generous with their caring. Actress Lindsay Wagner, a longtime friend, spoke wise and comforting words. When I said, "I feel like an old coat that's been hung up on a peg," she emphatically rejected that image. "You're not the old coat," she said firmly. "Your marriage is the old coat. You can let that be hung up on a peg."

The years of working side by side with my husband were over. Bill left our home. I left our clinic. I confronted the frightening question: What was I, a seventy-year-old woman, to do with the rest of my life?

As it turned out, that was the easy question. I was going to practice medicine, of course. The more difficult question was how and where I was going to do that. Our daughter Helene, who is also a doctor, was a great blessing in helping me find an answer. Together, we began a practice in Scottsdale. Setting up a medical office, however, is neither easy nor inexpensive, and financing our venture initially posed a problem. Banks are somewhat leery of lending money to a seventy-year-old divorcée, but I was fortunate to have a patient who could help—and desperate enough to ask him to co-sign a loan. He believed in us. We put ourselves in debt for $100,000 and went to work. There were patients to be seen and a busy practice to manage and, one day at a time, I survived many painful months.

One day in 1992, I learned that Bill was going to marry Peggy, the nurse who had been with us for more than twenty years. I was overwhelmed and shattered. I left the office, got into my car, and began the forty-five-mile drive home, but I had bottomed out emotionally. For the only time in my life, I totally lost control. Crying and speeding recklessly, I talked to God about the miseries in my heart. Peggy had Bill, Peggy had the clinic, Peggy had the work that Bill and I created together. It was unfair! I raged about the abuses heaped upon me until, finally, the emotional storm subsided. I pulled off the roadway and just sat in my car for a few moments, feeling drained and sad.

Then, from somewhere in the depths of my soul, came my father's message. He had always been steadfast in his admonition, "Do what you can and take comfort that whatever the outcome, you gave it your best."

I dried my tears, blew my nose, started the engine, and started home, talking now to myself. "Gladys, you are a fool. She may have all those things, but she will never be Gladys McGarey." I had given my marriage my best, and I could accept this outcome. Life stretched ahead of me with great promise, as it always had. "I will do what I can and I will give it my best," I told myself.

Had Bill found what he sought with Peggy? Perhaps. But perhaps he knew that he had also lost some good parts of his life. He stayed in touch with our children and wrote to me from time to time before he died. In one letter he said, "I want you to know I still love you and send you my greetings, and it would be great to hear from you that you have discovered forgiveness in regard to me."

I responded to Bill with gratitude and forgiveness. I made a detailed list that included:

I continue to thank you . . .

1) *For giving me your love. It's sad to me it didn't last;*

2) *For giving me wonderful children who have grown up to serve God and mankind;*

3) *For giving me precious special moments such as lying in your arms as we watched the sunrise in Rio Rico; and*

4) *For giving me a chance to go on and do
   my work as God is directing me to do
   it. It has been hard to understand, but
   now I know that you have given me my
   freedom. It was not what I wanted, but
   I believe it was what I needed.*

I read somewhere recently that if one creates
a beautiful tapestry but fails to hem it, the tapestry
can unravel. But it *can* be hemmed with gratitude. My
marriage to Bill and our life together created a beautiful tapestry, but it can unravel unless I hem it with
thanks. I don't want it to unravel. I don't want it to be
destroyed. What we did together was beautiful, and it
can go on as we go our separate ways.

We came a very long way together and we had
a good life. The memories are forever. The love we
shared is a living, holy thing. Our work in the field of
medicine has borne, and is bearing, fruit and changing
the face of medicine. Life is precious.

And life has gone on. I continue to practice
medicine, confident that the divorce, even with its pain
and my resistance, is part of the overall plan for my
life. I am thankful for each day with both its shadows
and its sunshine. The Himalayan Mountains taught me
that the beautiful mountain peaks would not exist if
there were no valleys. Life is good.

Our grandson Taylor was in my home the summer he was four. We were playing the game, "I spy
with my little eye . . . something that is green." Taylor,
along with the rest of us, was trying to guess what it

was. A few gave up, but Taylor said, "I never give up." After a while, someone else gave up, but again Taylor said, "I never give up." After another rather long while, he jumped down off the chair, ran around and around the living room, climbed back up on the chair and announced, "I will take a rest, but I will never give up."

Ah, Taylor, you are wise beyond your years. I will remember that there are times in life when I need to take a rest, but I won't give up.

Love Is Irrational

Bobbi Gibb

Seek the wisdom
that will untie your knot
seek the path
that demands your whole being.
Leave that which is not, but appears
to be
seek that which is, but is
not apparent.

—RUMI,
Rumi: Hidden Music

When I was a child, I followed my heart. I did what I loved to do: I ran. As I grew older, even though it was socially unacceptable in the fifties, I never stopped running. I ran with my dogs through the woods. Going into the woods was like entering a sacred temple. I felt a divine presence in nature that I felt nowhere else in my suburban existence of streets and roads. A run in the woods took me back to something very deep: a sense of an ancient, lost, and mystical communion with the sacredness of the earth.

It was in 1964 that I first heard about the Boston Marathon. I went to see it with my dad. I was mesmerized watching men who had integrated the ancient physical action of running on the earth into modern life. I felt the quiet, patient endurance and vision that it takes to run twenty-six miles, and I knew at that moment that I was going to run the Boston Marathon.

I started to train, even though I had no idea how. There were no running clothes for women. I had nurse's shoes and I wore a one-piece bathing suit under my shorts. I began to run longer and longer distances, not knowing whether my ability or my heart could carry me twenty-six miles. I tried to run the eight miles from Winchester, where I lived, to the School of the Museum of Fine Arts in Boston, where I was studying sculpture. I set goals for myself and gradually extended the distance. Soon, I was ranging all around Greater Boston on foot. It gave me an incredible sense of freedom and independence to go anywhere I wanted to go on my own two feet. "Oh, you want to go to Boston? Sure . . . ," and you run to Boston.

In the summer, with my Volkswagen bus and

my malamute puppy Moot, I traveled across the whole continent, running every day in a different place and sleeping at night out under the stars. I'd never seen the country. I wanted to see what land looked like that had never been touched by human beings. I wanted to feel it.

Moot and I ran the Berkshires of Massachusetts, the Adirondacks in New York, and the Appalachian Mountains of Pennsylvania and West Virginia. I ran across the Midwest in Ohio, Indiana, and Illinois, rejoicing in the fertile farmland. I crossed the Mississippi River at Hannibal, Missouri, and ran out across the Great Plains states—Kansas and Nebraska. At night, I made a nest of tall grass and lay looking up into the universe, feeling as if I were a water droplet hanging off the bottom of the earth.

In Colorado, Moot and I ran in the Rocky Mountains, way out in the wilderness. I was getting stronger and stronger. I could run fifteen miles and more at a stretch. I'd range like an animal, feeling my own wild nature. Moot, who was part wolf, felt it too. We went into Wyoming and down through Utah. I felt as if I were following some vast, benign, invisible power of creation that was everywhere, in everything, causing it to be. I was filled with wonder.

In Nevada, I followed a little dirt road and parked at the top of a mountain. I watched the sunset a thousand miles across the sky: pink, yellow, orange, purple, mauve, then deep indigo. The light evaporated from the sky as night fell and stars came out one by one. I'd never seen so many tiny sparks of light. There were more stars than dark places, unimaginable numbers cascading outward into the far reaches of the sky. It was a miraculous moment, floating in the vast infinity of time and space and I wondered, "How did all this get here, and why?"

After returning east, still training, I ran sixty-five miles of the hundred-mile equestrian event in Woodstock, Vermont. In January of 1966, longing to be near the Pacific Ocean, I moved to San Diego and finished my training on the beaches and mountains around Del Mar. I ran miles along the beach with the ocean crashing in huge, long, foaming breakers beside me. I ran to the top of Black Mountain and back, about twenty miles, feeling this running as the expression of my joy in being alive, feeling the wonder of all existence around me like a loving presence.

Then I knew I was ready.

In February 1966, I wrote requesting an application to run the Boston Marathon. I received a letter from Will Cloney, the race director, saying that women were not allowed to run it because women were not physiologically capable of running twenty-six miles. In fact, by the rules that governed international sports, women were not allowed to run more than one-and-a-half miles.

When I was told I couldn't run the Marathon, I chuckled and said, "Well then, they have something to learn! I'll run twenty-six miles and change the way everybody thinks about women. It will be a big joke!

Everybody thinks the world is flat? I'll show them it's round!"

I will always remember the ride on the bus from San Diego to Boston. A big, beautiful black woman from Watts sat next to me. She told me about the Watts Towers and how Watts was going to burn. We also talked about the civil rights movement. I fell asleep next to her. When I woke up, I felt something heavy and soft on top of me and I realized that she put her coat over me during the night because she thought I was cold. I looked over and watched her sleeping. I have never forgotten her.

The Vietnam War was going on. Lyndon Johnson was president and we were fighting the war on poverty. Bob Dylan and Joan Baez were entertaining us with songs. The women's movement hadn't really started; NOW (the National Organization for Women) hadn't even been formed yet and there was very little consciousness about women's rights.

When I arrived in Boston, I called my parents and they thought I had gone crazy—as usual—but my mother cooked a big dinner of roast beef and apple pie for me. My father was very angry. He was afraid that I had lost touch with reality. He left the house and as he did, he told me I was not allowed to run the marathon. He was worried. He was afraid I would hurt myself, but I persuaded my mother to drive me to the start of the race anyway.

My mother had lived her whole life never do-ing what she wanted to do. I convinced her that it was important for me to help women go beyond limits that were set for them. So she drove me to the start of the race in Hopkinton and dropped me off.

I still had an hour or more before the race started. I needed to warm up, after a four-day bus trip, so I ran two or three slow miles up and down an alleyway behind some buildings. It was almost noon, nearly starting time. I hid in the bushes. The gun fired and the men began to run. When about half the pack had moved out, I jumped in the middle. To conceal my long, blonde hair, I pulled the hood of my sweatshirt over my head. I knew at some point I had to reveal that I was a woman, but my fear was that police would stop and arrest me and I would not have a chance to prove that women could run.

I am very shy and nervous about getting up in front of people, and suddenly it dawned on me that I was going to be running in front of hundreds and thousands of people. I didn't know how people would react. Would they boo and hiss and throw me out? But love is irrational and love casts out fear.

It didn't take long for the men behind me to say to each other, "Is that a girl?" so I turned around and smiled. To my great relief, they were delighted. If they had been hostile, they could have called the officials or simply shoved me out. They said, "I wish my girlfriend would run," "I wish my wife would run," and "We think it's great that you are running." Alton Chamberlain, a tall, lanky man from Connecticut ran beside me to show his support. His presence gave me comfort.

"I'm getting hot," I told my fellow runners. "But if I take off my sweatshirt and they see I'm a woman, I'm afraid they will throw me out."

"It's a free road," they said. "We won't let them throw you out!"

So I took off my sweatshirt and threw it away. A boy in the crowd roared out, "It's a woman!" The crowd applauded and laughed. The women were screaming, the men were clapping, and the police said, "'Atta go, girlie!"

Reporter Jerry Nason from Winchester spotted me very early in the race. He began calling the news ahead of my arrival, so as I got closer to Boston, people were lining up to see me.

I ran to Wellesley, a women's college at roughly the halfway mark. When the students caught sight of me, they screamed, shrieked, jumped up and down, and cried. It was a ritual every spring. In those days, the women would make a kind of tunnel for the runners to pass through by standing in two parallel lines and waving their hands over their heads. The men loved it. "This is the best part of the race, seeing all these beautiful women," they said. Off to one side, an Italian woman stood holding a baby, with children clinging to her ample coat. When she saw me, she started yelling, "Ave Maria! Ave Maria!" Tears were running down her face, and many of the women were crying. That's when I started to cry, too.

I was running a mile in less than seven minutes. At that pace, I would finish in less than three hours. But

I didn't know that I was supposed to drink water. In high school I was told not to. I'd been warned I would get cramps, so even though everybody was offering me water and orange slices, I was politely refusing them. By the time I got to mile twenty, I was severely dehydrated, the bottoms of my feet were burning, my painful blisters were raw, and my pace had dropped off. The last couple of miles took me longer than the preceding eight. I just kept putting one foot in front of the other. And I thought, "By the time I get to the finish line, everybody is going to be gone."

I began to feel like a failure. This was not one of my better runs. And this is where I learned the real meaning of fortitude: To keep on even though your hopes are crushed.

The run became interminable as I slogged through Kenmore Square. Finally, as I turned right onto Dartmouth Street, everybody was hanging out of the windows screaming, "It's a girl!" as if I'd just been born. I turned left onto Boylston Street and the crowds let out a roar.

There were thousands of people. They weren't gone! They were packed in the grandstands and they were cheering. I picked up my pace and trotted over the finish line. The male runners were thrilled that I had finished. Alton wrapped his arm around me. The press trucks were there. The governor of Massachusetts, John Volpe, shook my hand. Some kind soul threw a blanket around me and I was rushed off to a nearby hotel where the press interviewed me. They told me that I'd finished in a time of about three hours and twenty minutes, ahead of two-thirds of the men. I was filled with joy.

When at last I arrived home, the house was filled with reporters. My poor parents were standing in the living room looking completely bewildered, as if to say, "What has she done now and what will she do next?" Their friends were calling and congratulating them. My dad was proudly telling everyone, "We knew she could do it!"

I put my arms around him and said, "Well, Dad, I guess it's those Gibb legs that I inherited from you!"

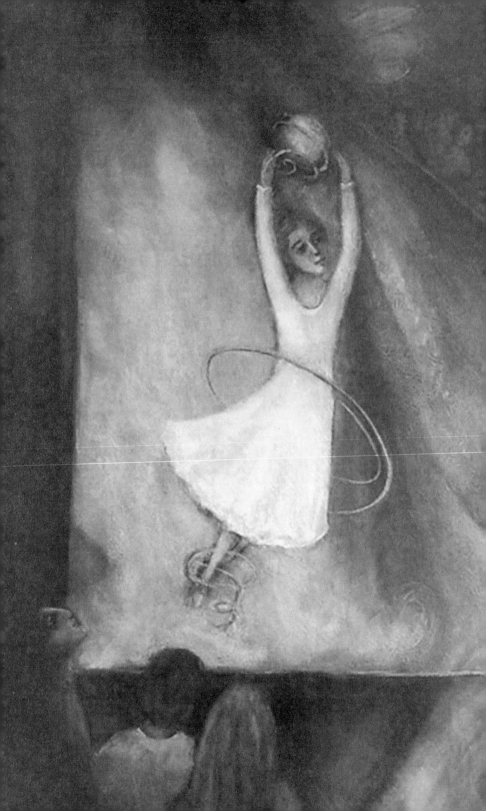

THREE

The Gift
in the Challenge

Just when the caterpillar thought the world was over, it became a butterfly.

—Anonymous

Receiving each experience as something that is happening for us, rather than something that is happening to us . . . allows us to grow and expand in ways we never imagined.
—JONELLE REYNOLDS,
spiritual counselor

The beauty in this chapter's stories lies in the women's ability to find a gift in the times they are besieged in their life. The reality of loss, illness and grief can be daunting, yet each woman goes beyond fear to harvest gold from the dark corners. Turning to prayer, dance, visualizations and inner strength, they find ways to comfort themselves and bring peace in the midst of crisis. Whether the crisis is death, catastrophic illness, oppression and suffering, or the hope to gain insight and grace for the onset of aging, each woman finds a place of comfort.

Faith, in knowing that they belong to God, sustains each woman as they find their own revelations, connections to spirit, or blessings in the circumstances that threaten them. On their unique mystical paths, they traverse to places where the outcome is unknown, but like all great seekers of light and truth they endure and expand. Even in facing adversity and extreme conditions they have the faith to believe that they are never ever beyond God's love.

The Porch

Kristi Meisenbach Boylan

"I don't know" is my favorite position.

—BYRON KATIE,
Loving What Is

A developmental milestone is reached some-where in early adolescence when we, as young women, first realize that our parents don't know everything. It's a turning point of sorts, the first of many autonomous awakenings, where we begin to move away from what is certain to what is not.

Years later, most of us pass another milestone as we become mindful of the fact that not only do our parents *not know* as much as we thought they did, but *we* don't know as much as we thought we did, either.

Even more life-changing is that third threshold of awareness, sometimes reached in our later years, sometimes never reached at all, when we are forced to concede that we can never, ever, be certain about anything, or anyone. Not even ourselves.

I fought the fate of the unknown for years—decades, really. I became educated, spiritually aware, socially sensitive, and politically active. I bristled at the thought of being uninformed. I read, studied, and analyzed. I became a perpetual student of everything. With the Internet and the non-fiction book industry at its peak, becoming an expert on life seemed so easy. The promise of enlightenment was on every corner.

I was most confident in the areas of menopause, parenting, and hyper kids. I interviewed doctors and specialists. I memorized data and statistics. I fought my way through a hellish ten years of fluctuating hormones, and raised one incredibly hyperactive child. I even wrote three well-received books on the subjects. At one time, I was sure I knew everything on these topics. My aplomb in my own wisdom was my security blanket.

Until I began to see the holes in my own story.

Suddenly, everything that had previously seemed like a sure thing wasn't. The minute I finished writing a book on how to move through menopause gracefully, I was smack dab back in it, mood swings and all. The minute I figured out how to wrangle an ADHD child without using medicine, the kid grows up and decides to take Ritalin.

After a lifetime of being tethered to a state of pretentious clarity, I found myself adrift in a sea of instability. The assurance of being anchored to my own inner wisdom disintegrated into the realization that *nothing* is certain. No matter how hard I worked at directing myself, my family, and my job, the nagging suspicion that I had somehow lost my mojo set in.

An even larger question loomed about the Divine. This feeling of overwhelming doubt went against my natural tendency to rely on my faith to get me through the tough times. My entire foundation, as well as my profession, was built around the principle of Divine Order. If I couldn't be certain about anything, where did God and my lifetime of devotion to faith and predictability fit in?

I've heard other women call reaching this point in their life as "hitting the wall." I have heard many others say it is being cynical or losing faith, referring to it as a shadow or valley in their life. But, again, I knew my shadows, and I had walked the valleys many times. This was different.

I likened it to a "spiritual meltdown" because, if you know anything about the Texas heat, you know that it has the tendency to melt everything in sight, even your spirit. My meltdown came on one such day. It arrived in the middle of summer and stayed for the fall and most of the winter. It presented itself as depression, but insecurity in my abilities as a mother, a wife, and—most of all—as a writer became the focal point of my misery. It was a time when I not only reached the end of my rope; I discovered there was no rope to begin with.

I ended up taking to my porch the way some women take to their beds in time of stress. For days on end, I sat in a lounge chair in one-hundred-plus-degree heat and sweated out my insecurities.

I am blessed to live on acreage, and my back-yard is a forest with a small stream running through it. Soon, my porch became my lifeline to nature and all that I could not harness with my intellect. And so it was there on my porch, under the heat of the Texas sun, that I dissolved. It's where I became the soupy mess that becomes of caterpillars waiting to turn into butterflies, and my lounge chair became the cocoon that cradled it.

Over the coming months, the leaves turned col-ors and dropped from the trees, filling the small stream beneath them. Christmas came and went, and still I sat on my porch. At one point, my husband even asked if we should move the bed into the backyard.

While it all sounds very Zen, very relaxing, it was not. I was eaten up by mosquitoes, stung by a yel-low-jacket wasp, and marauded by a swarm of June bugs. It was a slow, agonizing death in which all that I had known for sure about my life, my career, and my spirit oozed out of my pores and puddled on the tiled patio beneath my lounge chair.

After years of being strong, confident, and in control, I was horrified that my life had come down to this: one big, sweaty jumble on the back porch of my life.

I tried to read, hoping it would breathe some life back into me. I clung to the deflated life jackets of perceived knowledge that had been thrown my way in the form of books. I listened to myriad tapes of know-it-all commentators who claimed to have a patent on how to make me whole again—until I noticed that they, too, were wafting. The agony continued. I was not on top of my game. I probably never was. I was floundering emotionally and spiritually, and there was no way to find my footing. At one point, I wondered if I might ever write again.

The final resolution came one clear evening, as I watched the clouds drift over the moon. It was the beginning of April, and still cool enough that I had wrapped myself in a blanket. My beloved grandmother had just died, and I desperately wanted to feel like there was some meaning to life, and to all the misery I was feeling.

I pulled my chair off the porch and out in the yard toward the trees, closed my eyes, and listened from my cocoon for anything that resembled my grandmother's voice. The whisper that came was not from my grandmother, though, but from somewhere deep inside me. It started as a question in my gut, a wondering of "what if I really don't snap out of this? What if I have to live like this forever?" While horrified that I might never return to normal, it hit me that this might be my new normal, and if so, what would I do?

There was only one possible answer: I would

have to embrace God from within this darkness, and stop worrying about ever regaining my light.

That evening under the blanket of stars, I realized that the abyss I was experiencing was not the problem, it was the solution. Embracing the dark unknown was the only way out of the mess that I had gotten myself into.

The minute I surrendered completely to all that I did not, could not, and probably would not ever know, my spirit began to stir.

What I've learned from my year of being a soupy mess is that God exists in the most ambiguous spaces. I found Him on my back porch, in the dark. It was in these in-between moments in my chair, watching the trees, where nothing seemed solid, nothing predictable, that I found a Divine peace I have never known before.

I've also learned that while a few of us may experience the Divine in sparks of enlightenment or moments of joy, most of us experience the Divine like I did, when we need it most. We find it while we are suspended in the uncertainty of life, cocooned in bathtubs or couches, carpools and cubbies. And yes, sometimes the back porch.

Out of Sorrow

Eve Strella

Perhaps they are not the stars, but rather openings in heaven where the love of our lost ones pours through and shines down upon us to let us know they are happy.

—INUIT PROVERB

The day David died was cold and snowy with brilliant sunlight streaming through the patchy, dark gray clouds—a typical fall day in Rochester, New York. It was Wednesday, November 23, 1994, the day before Thanksgiving, and David was heading to the operating room for a second open-heart bypass surgery. His first bypass was nine years prior, and the five grafts had served him well. When he had his first bypass at age thirty-five, we both knew that additional surgery over the course of his life was pretty much guaranteed. We had been married for twenty-two years, and had been together for twenty-five years. We cherished every moment together, and our love for one another had gotten stronger and more intense with each passing year. He was my soul mate, my love, my best friend and reason for living—and I was his.

David had had an angiogram a week earlier and his doctor had kept him in the hospital until surgery could be performed. Needless to say, not being sent home was the first indicator of the severity of David's condition. Because we had been down the bypass road before, we went into this surgery confident that all would be well. We kept kidding each other, saying "piece of cake" when referring to the surgery and recovery.

When David and I left the house on the morning of the angiogram, neither of us realized that that was the last time he would see our beautiful home. In the days before the surgery, I lived every second I could at his side in the hospital. I would curl up in the recliner next to him. We would hold hands, watch TV, laugh, kiss, and hug. The nurses who caught us during loving moments would always comment on our affection and devotion. They said it was something they didn't see every day.

On the day of David's surgery, I arrived at the hospital at about 5:30 AM. I wanted to spend as much time with him as possible before he went to pre-op. He had been taken off all his medications in preparation for the operation, and during the night, his gout had returned with a vengeance. David was in severe pain in both feet. Since he could not take painkillers orally, I rubbed his feet to ease his pain, and he was very thankful for that. As he proceeded to pre-op, David was much more comfortable because of the drugs the pre-op staff had injected in preparation for surgery. The staff allowed me to stay with David up until the last moment before surgery.

Minutes before it was time for David to go to the operating room, he looked up at me with the most joyful smile on his boyish face and said passionately, "Thank you. Thank you for everything." A chill ran through me like a knife. It was the chill of reality. In my innermost core, I knew that he was thanking me for our life together.

At that instant, I knew that I would never see him alive again, that these were our final moments together. Immediately my coping mechanism kicked in. I consciously shook off the feeling deep in my gut. I smiled back at him and said, "Oh, David, if you think I have taken good care of you the last many days, you just wait till I get you home." A large part of me blocked the reality of losing David from my consciousness.

Pointing at the ceiling and laughing, David said, "The lines are moving." I looked up at the ceiling and saw nothing. I reassured David that nothing was moving and that the medication was making him see things. He replied, "No, no . . . look, they're moving. Don't you see them moving?" David continued to laugh and point upward as the staff wheeled him down the hall to the operating room. That was the last time we spoke, the last time I saw him alive and conscious.

I did not realize until long after David's death, when I was well along on my spiritual journey, what David meant by "the lines are moving." I came across a book written by hospice nurses who told of people transitioning over as they approached death. The first episode in the book addressed the most common scenario that the nurses witnessed, that of "the lines are moving" and the need for that person to get in line. The lines were formed by people in a queue, souls transitioning from the physical to the spirit. David had been transitioning right before my eyes, but I had written it off as a medication-induced delusion. My coping mechanism and lack of spiritual understanding would not allow me to see what was really happening—that David was dying and this was our end.

David was in the operating room for what seemed like forever. Every time I asked how he was doing, I was told that he was still in the operating room. I knew it was long past the hours needed to complete the operation. In my gut, I knew something had gone wrong. I paced the waiting area like a cat, anxious for someone to tell me that all had gone well, but the hours just went on and on. The doctor finally came out to tell me that they could not get David's heart started and that the situation was "grave." He also told me that if David survived, he would need a heart transplant. I pleaded with the doctor to save his life. I told him that

David was an engineer and a fabulous person, loved and respected by everyone, and that I could not live without him. I pleaded and pleaded with the surgeon to save him, to bring him back to me.

The next many hours are a blur. I cried and begged with the doctor, and with God, to save David's life. I begged for mercy. I asked for the Divine to grant me guidance, wisdom, and strength to survive emotionally. I remember a deafening silence, the pain of an unbearable reality and intense loneliness even though I was surrounded by people. My entire body went numb. About 4:00 PM, a nurse took me up to surgical ICU and escorted me in to see David. He was in an area isolated from other patients. There were so many tubes, pumps, and monitors. It all translated to the "grave" situation that the doctor had communicated in the waiting area. David was unconscious and non-responsive. A machine was breathing for him, and an artificial heart was pumping blood to keep him alive.

The doctors, nurses, and other support staff would not make eye contact with me. It was so odd. Why wouldn't they look at me? In hindsight, I understood. A glance from any of them would have conveyed the hopelessness of the situation.

I got as close to David as possible and sang to him, "I love you, puss cat, oh yes I do. I love you, pussy cat, with love so true. When you're not near to me, I'm blue. Oh, puss cat, I love you." I had to trust that David could hear me, and so I stayed very positive. When I returned to the waiting area, a clergyman was there. I knew he had come to console me and to give David his last rites. My heart sank. The situation was far worse then I had allowed myself to believe. Any hope that David might come home was shattered.

At 8:00 PM, the doctors took David back into surgery to try to stop the bleeding. Their attempts were unsuccessful. At 10:00 PM, a nurse came out. Grabbing me by the shoulders and shaking me, she said that things had taken a turn for the worse and that the doctor was coming in to talk with me. At that point, life as I had known it dissolved. All had changed—forever. The doctors could not stop the bleeding. They had used all the blood of David's type in the Rochester area. After I said goodbye to David, they were going to disconnect all life support. My emotions had shut down and I felt utterly numb. I was in a state of total disbelief. I wanted so much to wake up from this nightmare. As I was escorted to David's bedside, I removed the name card from the ICU wall that said "Strella, David." Why I did this, I have no idea.

When I went to his bedside, I put my cheek on his forehead and calmly told him that the doctors had done all they could do and that I needed to let him go. Surrounding David was all the equipment keeping him alive. I could hear all the pumps and the beeping of the monitors. But now I heard a new sound— a gurgling sound in David's chest. After the second surgery, the surgeon had not closed David's chest, and so this rhythmic gurgling was clearly audible above all the other sounds. This gurgling was the sound of

David's heart beating, kept alive by the pumping of the artificial heart. I sang him my puss cat song and continued to tell him that I had to let him go. How I knew to give him permission to die is beyond me. When I told David for the third time that I had to let him go, there was a profound silence. All at once, the equipment stopped. The artificial heart, the respirator, the auditable on the IVs, and the gurgling in David's chest—all stopped. I stood straight up, knowing that something devastating had just happened. As I looked at the monitor, the line went flat and all values went to zero. Because my emotions were so shut down, I couldn't register what had just happened, and so I put my cheek back on his forehead and continued to sing to him. But he was gone. It was 10:21 PM and my "pussy cat" David was dead.

As I left the hospital that night, I instinctively reached my hand back, looked over my shoulder and, in a whisper, asked David to come with me, to come home. That night, David had done two things for me: He waited to hear my voice one more time, and he stopped the equipment so that I wouldn't have to live with the thought that, when I walked away, all life support would be disconnected, leaving me feeling guilty for his death. To this day, I don't understand how all the equipment could have stopped. Electricity was powering all the life support. I did not trip over a plug or disconnect anything. The staff was nowhere near David's bed to turn anything off. This had to have been due to the power of our love and the power of the human spirit. David had shut down the equipment to make it easy for me.

The year following David's death was something I would never wish on anyone. I was constantly sick and depressed. With no family in the area, I relied on supportive phone calls from my sister in New Jersey, and on moral support and hugs from my dear Rochester friends. I was terrified that I would lose everything that David and I had worked so hard for: our home, our savings. As crazy as it sounds, I was even afraid of losing my job. You name it and I was afraid it would disappear. I created a central location on my dining room table for all paperwork: bills, documents dealing with the estate, death certificates—everything. I called this my "widow's table." Because David had handled all household matters, I found myself working hard to gain an understanding of what needed to be paid and by when.

Every day was a living hell for me. When I got home from work, I would start searching for David. I reasoned that he had to be in the house somewhere, so I would go room to room in search of him. If he wasn't in the living room, then he had to be in the dining room, or in the kitchen or upstairs. This searching took place every night for six months. When I finally accepted that David was no longer in the house, I could still feel his strong spiritual presence in every room.

I am the person I am today because of David Strella: strong, confident, and optimistic. David's death was the starting point of my spiritual journey. Never before did I need to understand where a person's physical and spiritual energy goes when that person dies. But with David's death, I needed to know; I needed to understand. I began reading countless books on the loss of a loved one. I learned silence and meditation. I began two journals: a detailed journal of daily events and a dream journal of every dream in which David appeared. I attended inspirational lectures. I joined an astronomical society to expand upon my love of stargazing and increase my knowledge of the universe. I started listening to New Age music; it not only lifted my spirit, but also inspired creativity and intellectual growth. And I went through a spiritual healing in Mexico that clearly illustrated to me how much of me was on the other side with my husband. It seemed that every time I was ready for the next step in my healing process, the books and people—everything—that I needed would appear in my life.

On my spiritual journey, I found the courage, determination, and inspiration that I needed, not only to carry on, but also to succeed in my new life. This path has brought me to where I am today. I have an incredible relationship with my new husband, Ed, whom I met at an astronomy meeting. I never thought I would fall in love again, but I have found that it is possible to have more than one soul mate in a lifetime. Ed and I love spending time together observing the moon, stars, and universe as we snuggle under the dome of Stardust, our private observatory and temple to the cosmos.

I have learned so much on this journey. Now I know that events in life happen for a reason, no matter how painful at the time. I have also learned that there are no coincidences in this life, and so I pay close attention to causal encounters and events. I've learned to drink in every experience and vista, to savor every color, to laugh loud and often, until tears roll down my face. I tell those who are important in my life how much I love them. Ed and I hold hands, kiss, and snuggle at every opportunity. I have learned that life is over in a heartbeat, to cherish every moment . . . and I do.

The Gift

Alison Norman

There are many paths to the light in this glittering, healing, dancing world.

—TERRY LÁSZLÓ-GOPADZE

"Hold on. Hold on to yourself. Because this is going to hurt like hell."

Sarah McLachlan's song played on the radio in my room as if she were singing directly to me. I repeated the lyrics in my head, over and over as I lay in bed, wishing I could return to the naïve young girl I had been last week.

But today, as I ran my fingers through my long, blonde hair, I began to lose my identity with every strand that fell out. I was frightened, scared *to* death and scared *of* death. Consumed by my own hell, I sang and cried, never once able to get through the song in its entirety without breaking down. The vicious cancer—my cancer—was trying to conquer not only my body, but also my spirit. Looking for something familiar, I searched my room for evidence of the person I used to be. I found a picture of myself taken only a few weeks earlier: a young, healthy, twenty-year-old girl with long, curly blonde hair stared back at me with a smile. I envied her. I longed to be that girl again.

Before the chemotherapy for ovarian cancer could take control of me, I grabbed the scissors and anxiously began to cut. Like the character Demi Moore played in the movie *G.I. Jane*, I, too, shaved my head in preparation for war. As I removed the last remnants of my hair, I felt a surge of power fill my body. In that minute, I no longer felt like a victim of a life-threatening disease, but an active participant in a struggle that was to define who I was and who I would become. My first maneuver on the battleground was to learn how to survive.

Shaving my head was lesson one.

At times, I would forget that I didn't have hair. Then, I would walk in front of a mirror and get a glimpse of myself and fail to recognize the person staring back at me. I received a picture drawn by a child I baby-sat. This little girl, only four years old, depicted both of us in beautiful, flowing dresses with bright smiles on our faces and her hand in mine. She had long hair and I had none; there was our difference, defined in pastels. It hurt me to look at the card. It was then I recognized that others also had a difficult time adjusting to my new look. I found myself saying, "I am still the same person you have always known. I am Ali. You know me. I haven't changed." I was hoping I could believe it myself.

In order to survive the pity I saw in everyone's eyes, I tried to make jokes about being bald. I would tell stories about how I scared my cat. But in the end, I made the children I loved and baby-sat for cry and made adults look the other way. Sometimes, I would put my wig on backwards or only half way on in an effort to authenticate my disease and hide from it at the same time. Although my efforts brought a few laughs, I could still see concern in my loved ones' eyes. I felt responsible for their worry. I needed them to know that I was going to be all right and that I could take care of myself. I tried to reassure others, although unfortunately, at times, I truly needed their help.

I have always valued my independence and been proud of the fact that I was able to pay for my car, college, and most of my food since I was a teenager. Because of cancer, I suddenly had to rely on others. I was raised by a single mother who loved me dearly, but who was forced to leave for work before I got out of bed. My mother taught me at the age of nine to be self-reliant. I learned to care for myself. I had to wake myself up, fix my own breakfast, get dressed, and walk to school. When I became ill, I was forced to move back in with my mother and have my meals prepared for me. I often needed help getting dressed. I had to be driven to the hospital for my daily shots. When the effects of my illness were really bad, I required someone to help me do the most basic functions. I fought against my own pride in order to accept the help I so desperately needed.

Hoping to escape my illness, if only in my mind, I begged my mother and two sisters to take me on a vacation. They obliged and we headed off to Ensenada, Mexico. Wearing my blonde wig, I appeared healthy and, for a while, the masquerade seemed to be the medicine I needed. For a few hours, I didn't feel like "the young girl with cancer," as people in my hometown would often refer to me. Instead, I felt like the girl I used to be. But by the end of our first night, the vacation medicine wore off and once again, the chemotherapy took control. I didn't want my family to worry or the vacation to end, so I tried to hide the fact that I wasn't feeling well. But alas, the charade was over; I woke up the next morning with my body feeling as if it were on fire.

Fearing the thought of a hospital stay in Mexico, my family rushed me back to the United States. My desire to escape the reality of my illness ended with my family and me imprisoned in bumper-to-bumper traffic for two solid hours. I crossed the border with a 103-degree fever while young children banged on the windows of my mother's car, trying to sell us Chiclets gum.

After finally reaching the hospital, we were all exhausted from our so-called vacation. I told my family I would be all right, and they left me in the hospital and returned home in the hope of getting a good night's sleep. I lay in my hospital bed, freezing cold and begging for blankets. Instead, I received a bath in ice cubes to halt the fever. I couldn't even enjoy the flowers my loved ones wanted to give, because my body couldn't fight off the natural bacteria such gifts would carry. I wanted to call my friends to vent and to be comforted by their voices, but my throat was too swollen to speak. Instead, I watched someone else's blood drip into my veins and stared at the clock, anxiously waiting for a visit from the nurse who would deliver my next morphine shot to calm the pain. Then I broke down and cried. I cried and cried for so many reasons: for losing my strength, my ovaries, my hair, and my innocence. I cried for myself and for all the women who had died, losing their personal battles with ovarian cancer. I cried and cried, and then I cried a little more. I was emotionally and physically exhausted, and began to question why I was fighting so hard—for at that moment, I felt as if I would rather be dead.

Then one of my best friends, Jennifer, a mentor and my spiritual teacher, came to visit me. She, too, had faced a life-threatening disease—and conquered it. Jennifer knew the remedy I needed most at that moment. I needed to believe in myself and in my strength and find my spirit. Her curly brown hair bounced on her shoulders as she moved closer to me. Her smile was as big as her heart, and as she sat by my bed, we laughed and we cried. And then she spoke to me with wisdom far greater than her years.

Jennifer brought me a music CD that her shamanic healer had given her. The music was meant to help, but the sounds of drums and Indian chanting frightened me. I asked myself why I was afraid, and remembered the words of my father, a born-again Christian minister: "Only Jesus has the power to heal. All other forces are guided by the devil."

I had been taught that yoga, meditation, and even martial arts were evil unless they gave credit to Jesus. Yet Jennifer firmly believed that she had been healed through the help of her shaman. She told me that my illness was a gift as long as I learned from it. She gave me a card. Written in her beautiful handwriting were these words:

> *Ali,*
>
> *You are on a journey that will take you places. The unknown will give you wisdom. The depth of this wisdom can not be described in words; it is just a "knowing." I believe that you have the inner power and courage to make this life a life of full light and sunshine. You will glow as the sun, for the warmth you possess will help you to overcome any obstacle that comes your way. Your spirit will soar.*

I understood Jennifer's words. I wanted to believe that my cancer would serve a positive purpose, not only in my life, but also in the lives of those around me. It was a strange feeling. And although I was scared and at times angry, I also began to believe that cancer—the cancer in my body—could teach me many powerful lessons and eventually assist me in helping others. My feeling of wanting to give up disappeared, and I regained my strength. Later, as I became more comfortable with holistic healing and new forms of spirituality, I began to practice yoga, meditation, and visualization. I realized there were many paths to God, and many names for God, even if they are not the traditional roads to which my father subscribes.

One day, Jennifer and I attended a meditation and dance class. When we arrived, I did not feel very well, so I watched while others danced. And then it happened. I felt a surge of energy when we were instructed to close our eyes and to envision our biggest goal. My goal was to be well again. I closed my eyes and imagined that I was well, that I was strong and healthy and cancer-free. We were asked then to dance as if that goal had been accomplished. As I stood up, I imagined my blonde hair caressing my skin as it fell around my neck and shoulders. I felt the cancer rise out of my body and disappear into the universe. No longer covered in the veil of cancer, I looked in the mirror and saw that my face was not swollen due to steroids. The bruises on my arms from constantly being poked by needles had also disappeared. There, in the world of my own universe, I danced as a strong woman who knew she could survive. In that moment, I saw myself as a woman who was not afraid to look back and, more importantly, was not afraid to look ahead.

Silently, I thanked God for the challenges He had placed before me. I envisioned my family staring at me, their eyes clear of the fear to which we had all become accustomed. They embraced me and told me they loved me and were proud of me. My friends were smiling, too. I could see the excitement in their faces, for now I was ready to join them and participate in a world filled with healing.

I realized that my beauty always shines because it comes from the inside. I danced with the group that had awakened my spirit and directed me to the path that would take me to my goal. And as I danced, I thanked them for their gift.

Encounter

Josefina Burgos

I once, suddenly and unexpectedly,
found myself in the presence of a God.
And She was as real as I am.
Now She dwells inside of me, strong and quiet.
I also know She is a part of the world.

Ever since I was a young child, I've had dreams filled with images of flying swiftly among the stars and in full control of my speed and direction; dreams in which I was filled with an extraordinary sense of exhilaration and joy. I experienced recurring dreams of flying in a summer night sky, looking down at my house in Santiago and the garden with its long row of poplars in the moonlight, engulfed in a sense of complete harmony with the universe—a perfect Chagall painting with its starry nights and hovering figures. I remember dreaming about the ocean; the beautiful, blue-green ocean I loved in my youth. I spent the summers at El Tabo, a small, humble resort on the central coast of Chile. Swimming and submerging in clear green waters, swaying up and down with the waves in a kind of oceanic ecstasy, I participated in a playful harmony with a nourishing entity. Feelings of connection, and belonging to something much bigger than myself, were ever-present.

My younger days were infused with this sense of connection, awe, and mystery. It was a feeling that, later on, was sadly suffocated by modern life: career, ambition, and competitiveness—the rat race. Eventually, the awe died, the mystery disappeared, and my life became dull and permeated by a bewildering sense of emptiness. The connection between the tangible world of my everyday life and the wonderful realm beyond my consciousness had been broken. So the story I am now about to tell is the story of a woman who, without being aware of it, experienced a dream-like relationship with the divine in her early life, lost it, and found it again through a traumatic experience of profound suffering.

I was born in Potrerillos, which means "Little Pastures," 11,500 feet above sea level in the Andes Cordillera. I remember huge full moons; transparent, crystalline air; vast, vast perspectives; and the delightful memory of my father carrying me on his shoulders.

He was a physician in the only hospital in Potrerillos, a little mining enclave owned by the Anaconda Copper Mining Company. Unfortunately, when the time came for my brother and me to go to school, we had to leave that magic realm of moonlight, thin air, and limitless views. We moved to Santiago, Chile's capital.

School, college, marriage, a baby son . . . all led to a peaceful, middle-class life in the midst of a large, Latino-like, nurturing family group. My life became a little too peaceful, maybe a little too boring. It was then that a feeling of emptiness crept over me, and life lost its wonder.

This peaceful way of life came to an abrupt end September 11, 1973, when a military coup deposed elected president Salvador Allende and destroyed the longstanding, proud Chilean democracy. Allende, who either was assassinated or committed suicide, was replaced with a military junta headed by General Augusto Pinochet. The days and nights of terror had begun.

My husband was an air force officer and, like many other military men, refused to act against the constitutional government and was taken prisoner. I did not know of his whereabouts for two long months, only that he was being held someplace and interrogated, tortured, and psychologically mistreated. When I was finally allowed to visit him, I could see the wounds made by the restraining devices on his wrists. There were other wounds, I knew, which I could not see— the wounds to his body and wounds to his soul. After his release from isolation, my husband and some of his air force colleagues were transferred to a public prison. I was allowed to visit him only once or twice a week.

One night after midnight, I was dragged away from my home and forced to leave my five-year-old son alone. I "disappeared," like the *desaparecidos* of Argentina, whose mothers gathered in protest in the Plaza de Mayo in Buenos Aires in an attempt to find their missing children. I was tortured, pushed to confess to actions prefabricated to fit the military political agenda, and forced to spend my time in complete isolation. I didn't know if I would survive or if I would ever see my son again. The thought of my little boy, my husband, and my parents' suffering made the emotional pain unbearable, and I reached a state of profound hopelessness, impotence, and terror. There was always the possibility of renewed torture that, apart from the physical suffering, was always sexually inspired and made death seem like a sweet deliverance.

I had abandoned a belief in God long before, the God of the Catholic tradition in which I had been raised, so praying was out of the question for me. I felt completely powerless and defeated; I had reached the bottom of hell. Eventually, I totally let go of myself, of my own suffering and destiny. Only one thing mattered and that was my child. He was alone, threatened, and there was nothing I could do for him. I could not bear to think of his life without his two parents, without my guidance and protection; I could not bear to think of him needing me and me not being there for him.

That's when I saw an imprint of a little child's

hand on the wall. I was facing the corner assigned to me in the room where I was kept when I noticed it— the outline of a little hand of a child about the age and size of my son's. The intensity of my pain seemed to explode and to leap beyond an invisible boundary, gradually transforming itself into an enormously powerful energy. I was suddenly aware of the immensity of my love for this child, my son; of the immensity and the power of the love of all mothers, human and non-human, for their offspring—a love like no other that can transcend the boundaries of humanity and ego.

Suddenly, I felt part of a force superior to me. I envisioned a Mother encompassing all of the mothers in the universe, and all the love and compassion of a creator for its creatures—an entity more powerful than me, who could understand my predicament and share my suffering. Then I was able to pray, and in a symbolic and mental ceremony, I handed my son's little hand to Her. In my impotence, I put him under Her protection. What followed was a profound sense of peace, then a sense of deep strength and mental control that, together, allowed me to endure the ghastly treatment I received until I was released.

Finally one day, after the military powers-that-be understood that there was nothing new I could possibly reveal to them, they put me in a pickup truck and took me home. It was the middle of a sunny December afternoon. The street where I lived was quiet and peaceful, completely unaware of the turmoil going on and of the blood being spilled in secret and dark places. I remember seeing a butterfly delicately land on a flower in my garden, as if nothing, nothing at all, had ever happened. I remember feeling the coolness of the soft breeze on my skin and then, in a daze, I remember seeing one of my friends turning the street corner holding my son's hand. My first impulse was to run and embrace him, and cry with big, loud, sobs, but then I stopped to soothe my heart and walked calmly toward them. I smiled and said hello to my friend. Then I hugged my son and asked him if he had had a good time while Mommy was away. He said he had and hugged me back. He was in a hurry to tell me all the wonderful things that he and my friend had done together. I closed my eyes and poured my soul into a thankful prayer.

Riley:
The Town I Almost Missed
(Or, Sheri and Mr. Fields
Go On a Vision Quest)

Sheri Ritchlin

i thank You God for most this amazing
day: for the leaping greenly spirits of trees
and a blue true dream of sky; and for everything
which is natural which is infinite which is yes.

—E.E. CUMMINGS,
"i thank You God for most this amazing"

If you believe in omens, omens were against it.

If you follow astrological transits, my convergence of Pluto, Mars, and Uranus transits said, "Beware."

If you were an *I Ching* scholar (I was writing my dissertation on it), it would have given you serious pause when the hexagram for Danger appeared.

If you have simple common sense, when a woman who is a wilderness backpacker, kayaker, and intrepid outdoorswoman told you that you were very courageous to undertake a trip from Montana to California in *that* (pointing to Mr. Fields), you'd take note. Especially if you are none of the above, and haven't driven in ten years. I didn't tell her that part. And I went anyway.

Mr. Fields and I set out in September, after a summer of dissertation writing, on a journey that was both a return and a vision quest. For young Native American men, a vision quest was a form of initiation from boyhood into manhood—a period alone in the wilderness, waiting for a dream, a vision, or a sign. Mr. Fields and I were hardly young initiates. I was a fifty-five-year-old woman and Mr. Fields was a 1972 "cabover camper," and we were on our way from Lolo, Montana, to Oakland, California. It was the year 2000 and the world was making its transition into a new millennium, as I was making that peculiar transition into old age that we never believe will happen. Take my word for it: it does. And it can happen very simply. In your forties or your fifties. Suddenly, a horizon drops down in front of you, cutting you off from the dream of endless future possibilities. You see yourself walking towards it, and you know inexorably that your step will fail in some way, suddenly or slowly. And you will come to the end of it. Nothing is infinite and eternal any more, as it is to the young initiate. So in a way, the mysteries are even deeper.

Old age is the secret crisis that no one is allowed to talk about. It was not so much that I was frightened—although, at first, I was indignant and enraged—but I was awed and challenged by it. I knew that I was approaching that turning point, that passage, and I simply wished to do it well. With grace, if possible. My vision quest in Mr. Fields was made with the hope of receiving a sign or a vision, a tiny arrow of meaning to point me in the direction of that grace. It was time to start sorting through the box that said, "Things I want to do in my life" and make some serious choices. My list was small but not modest. Get my PhD. Get the vision of my life, which I had been shaping in word and song for years, "out." Lift up my voice. Speak. Sing. If I didn't get those things out now, they would die inside of me and return to ashes.

I'm not sure why I felt a little strange and fatigued on the journey across Oregon from Vale to Burns. Driving conditions were better. The sun was shining. Perhaps it was the lingering effect of the harrowing journey over the Rockies, through icy passes in a big, unwieldy camper that crept up hills like a dying dog and plunged down them like a bolting bronco.

I decided that I would stop in Burns for lunch and would later pick up food for supper at a market in Riley. Chickahominy Campground was four miles beyond Riley and, at two dollars a night, fit the small budget that had grown smaller since my front brake seals had gone in Orofino, Idaho.

Once past the steeper passes, the road opened up into wide, flat, semi-desert country, and driving was easy. The wind was right. Mr. Fields got more easily into his fifty-five-mile-per-hour stride.

Too easily, perhaps.

I almost missed Riley.

I *would* have missed it if I hadn't seen the turn-off sign for U.S. Route 395. Suddenly, I couldn't remember if the campground was on 395 or 20. I slowed down and pulled over to check the map. Only there wasn't really a place to pull over. No shoulder, just a few inches, and then a drop into dark earth. Moments later, two behemoth trucks roared by me. With a shudder, I contemplated the danger of my action. I can't see the traffic behind me in Mr. Fields. What if one of them had been right on my tail? It brought to mind the gathering omens of danger that had almost caused me to delay my trip. Yet my intuition had said strongly that it was the time to go.

Early evening light was turning gold across the landscape as I stepped out of the truck to get my bearings. The land stretched out endlessly in all directions, though the subtle outline of mountains was still visible. Where was Riley?

I looked behind me and saw, across the street in the shadows, a low building with a parking lot in front. I turned the camper around and went in the small store to ask.

Yes, this was Riley. Yes, the Chickahominy Campground was four miles down the road. Yes, they had RV spaces but so did Riley. Right here. Five dollars without hook-ups. I was sure the Chickahominy Reservoir would be cheaper. And prettier. This was Nowheresville, a God-forsaken place. But expediency, the sight of 395 right there, heading directly off to my next destination, won out. That overpowering urge to stop that strikes the long-distance traveler was upon me.

As I drove into the little parking area behind the store, I saw the huge hand-painted sign, facing the opposite direction from which I had come: "WHOA!! YOU MISSED RILEY!" I had to laugh.

I woke up at six in the morning feeling much better. It was *cold*. When I lifted the metal door to light the pilot on my heater, a sharp little gust of wind came through so that it was difficult to light the match. I must have gone through a dozen of them, and even when it caught, the pilot went out before I could get the knob turned to "on." Finally it was lit, my coffee was made, and I climbed up into my loft bedroom-office-library. Still shaken by that close call on the highway, I decided that I would turn to the *I Ching* for counsel. What if it said, "Do not cross the great water"? Would that mean that I shouldn't proceed? And if it did, would I be willing to stay another day? The thought of staying another day in Riley was hard to face.

Reluctantly, I produced the coins and the book. I knew there was no turning back. And maybe it would surprise me, tell me there was no problem and I could continue on with great confidence. But that was not the case. The coins were cast. The answer was unequivocal: "It would not be advantageous to make a movement in any direction whatever." Yi Wu's comment on this was, "In a time of splitting, which means energy problems, the only way to act is to be cautious and to save your energy. When your energy increases or you start a great development of your work, you need to establish two brakes: moral rules and cultivation of desirelessness." (Hadn't I just replaced two brake seals?) The oracle's answer took me to the core; the deepest, truest issues. If one proceeds cautiously, reverently, correctly, danger—and even death itself—is entered in the right posture.

I sighed. Another day in beautiful downtown Riley that I almost missed.

Dreams, astrology, and the *I Ching*—like spiritual practice and religious observance—are features of the inner landscape and native to that world, that essential soil where outer actions, attitudes, and events are seeded. Many people would think I was crazy to stop over in Riley for such a thing. But looking back, I often think, "What if I hadn't?"

In honor of Mars, I decided to spend the extra time in physical activity, putting things in order. I rearranged cabinets and drawers, got in a new supply of water, and did small camper chores that felt very good. The release of that relentless forward momentum of a trip was relaxing. I felt good. The day was beautiful.

A lovely peace settled over me as the day went on. When the chores were finished, I gathered my maps and guides and studied the route before me. If I really considered this a vision quest, I could hardly omit a visit to Mt. Shasta, one of the sacred mountains of the world. This would surely be the peak experience of the trip.

I had parked Mr. Fields with the back door facing a small irrigation ditch. Directly opposite the door, at the edge of the ditch, was something like a dwarf willow tree. The scale of vegetation here was so much smaller, and the landscape so much more sparse, than the tall, green, majestic settings of Montana and Idaho, with their swift rivers, waterfalls, and wide clear lakes. The muddy little irrigation ditch and the pitiful little willow tree seemed poor cousins indeed. Yet throughout the day, I grew increasingly charmed by the shifting light of the landscape and the way the look and color of the small tree was constantly changing. I was amazed by the variety of birdsong I heard and the little tree played host to constant visitations of small flocks.

The sun had an unobstructed voyage through a clear blue sky from horizon to horizon. As it dropped toward the west, the bird activity seemed to increase. I had heard geese overhead during the day, but suddenly their clamor filled the air so steadily and noisily that I had to get out and have a look.

What a sight! Hundreds of them flying in out of the east and the northeast. One after another, the V-shaped flocks passed over, announcing their passage with that signature trumpeting call. As I looked to the left, I realized that they were flying very low and finally, that they were landing in a large field just across the highway from Mr. Fields. *They* weren't going to miss Riley!

I ran to get my binoculars and saw that they had formed a very long horizontal column across the field, like a phalanx of soldiers. They snacked and chattered in their individual platoons, but they were clearly under a larger command. The troops were still mustering and their ranks thickening as I turned back toward the camper, filled with the infectious sense and sounds of their camaraderie. It seemed to me that they were campers pausing in their journey on that side of the highway, just like those of us on this side in the small, bleak campground; fellow travelers, though they offered each other much more companionship than we did.

So this was how the day progressed and how Riley changed from a barren no-man's-land to a place of incredible richness and life. By the next day, my little willow even played host to a flock of meadowlarks. Energy transmuted into life, flight, song. The company of birds headed south. Desirelessness. To open emptily to the unexpected moment and to be filled with light.

It happened while I was standing in the camper, looking west out of the windows. In that horizontal landscape filled with sky, there was a crescendo of light that had turned the brown fields to warm gold and kindled the surface of the muddy irrigation ditch into a bright mirror. The small, narrow leaves of the willow were a translucent pale yellow, shivering with the darting arrival of small birds.

As I looked out, a soft wind blew across the water and the tips of the tiny waves caught the sun's light. It was like watching a burst of stars and I fell into a trancelike state, watching the sparks of light melt into a large radiant shape that shimmered against the blue sky. The figure of light grew, shifted, and danced like the shining presence of a god. And as it danced, something deep within me danced with it. A cosmic dance. Light and energy at the heart of the universe. Dancing. Alive. Shining.

Then a bracelet of diamond light appeared on the surface. So beautiful! A jeweled gift out of the depths of water. I shook myself a little. "That is just a fish," I reminded myself, "biting at an insect on the surface of the water. This is all a brilliant illusion created by a collection of things—the setting sun, the fish, the wind. . . ."

But then a voice said, "The fish, too, is just a collection of things, and it is no more or less an illusion than the ring of light. Each is a different collection of things, as is every creation, every phenomenon in the universe. What matters lies in how you collect and what you collect. That is your unique and distinctive choice. Your quality. And your individual reality."

I didn't go to Mt. Shasta. I thought no more about horizons. The turning had been made. I understood at last that I was the arrow of meaning and the bow was held in sure, invisible hands that would send me beyond where human eyes could see. My seeing was for here, for now, orchestrating the rich sights and sounds of daily life as beautifully as possible. And trusting that deep at the core of me, and of the universe, the invisible god was eternally dancing.

Five years later, you might think that a sixty-year-old woman would have settled into her comfort by now, contemplating her retirement, and living quietly with her memories. But that is just one collection of possibilities. I have chosen another. Five years have passed, and I still live in Mr. Fields. He has allowed me to press on toward the vision before me, and brought me a different, primordial sense of comfort. Still no hook-ups, but we are far from Riley and its hospitable little willow. We live, at least part of the time, on an organic vegetable farm in Sonoma County. We share the eucalyptus trees with great horned owls and red-tailed hawks and California orioles. We have a lovely view of Sonoma Mountain and vineyards on the hillsides. Every evening, I watch for the alchemical fire, the dancing cosmic light, the unexpected beauty in the unexpected places.

I completed my dissertation in Mr. Fields, crouched with my laptop under a piece of plastic to avoid a leak in the ceiling. But that's fixed now. After graduation, I completed my first published work, *One-ing*, inspired by a sight through Mr. Fields's skylight. Two magazine articles have been published since then and some songs recorded. I'm going down my list. Tomorrow I might live or die, but today is full of everything. Every moment is a Riley—a treasure on the verge of being lost.

It's all in how you put it together.

FOUR

Changes and Choices

When we surrender to the great unknown,
we choose to awaken gracefully.
Letting go of the past and what was,
allows us to open to one little miracle after another,
changing and calling us,
to trust the unknown and all that can be.

Faith is the bird that feels the light and sings when the dawn is still dark.

—RABINDRANATH TAGORE,
Fireflies

The women in this chapter have made changes and choices in exceptional ways. They each have an eternal perspective that serves as a bridge to opportunities. They transcend difficulties in surprising ways, as their obstacles become doors.

The core of the following stories may be an event that shatters daily life, or it may be a number of less visible, but no less desperate, circumstances that profoundly shake a woman's life. No simple solutions are available to meet them and no simple wisdom offers comfort. Yet each women encountered such a moment, and found in the depths of it the root of her own spiritual transformation.

These women of great spirit have chosen to go past whatever difficult situation has befallen or bewildered them. Each finds a way to focus on something good that surpasses her own suffering. Their tremendous optimism is based on faith, rather than circumstances, for the power of the mind can change a situation into a golden opportunity; it's all in the heart of the choice.

Changes

Nicolette Tal

Healing is not the same thing as curing, after all; healing
does not mean to go back to the way things were before,
but rather allowing what is now to move us closer to God.
—Ram Dass,
Still Here

For me, the physical process of writing involves twitching my lower lip very slightly to activate a laser placed precisely near the corner of my mouth. The laser, in turn, is hooked up to my laptop computer, which is equipped with special software that provides a menu of letters, numbers, symbols, and predicted words, highlighted in a regular pattern. When the letter or word or whatever I need is highlighted, I twitch my lip and it appears on the screen.

This is also the way I have conversations. The only voluntary muscles in my body that still work are my eyes and that little twitch of my lip. Although my vocal cords still can produce sound, I have very little control over the nature of the sound that comes out, and thus my vocalizations are hard to decipher.

In 1997, I was diagnosed with a motor neuron disease. We normally lump all motor neuron diseases together and call them amyotrophic lateral sclerosis, or Lou Gehrig's disease. But my wise and wonderful neurologist, on a shred of evidence that I might have a variant called multifocal motor neuropathy, decided to treat it as such and treat it aggressively. The hope generated by these efforts helped give my family and me the courage and strength to continue our lives as normally as possible right at the onset, when most patients and relatives are too overwhelmed by the diagnosis to carry on.

At first I had trouble turning a key, and I lost my ability to write or even use a regular computer very early in the disease's progression. I tried a variety of adaptive devices to feed myself, but one by one they failed, and I had to be fed by others. Then my arms and legs weakened and I began to fall frequently, especially off of curbs and over parking-lot speed bumps, but miraculously never breaking more than a toe. I tried wearing leg braces, but by the time they were made for me, I was ready for a wheel chair.

When I became ventilator dependent in May

1998, my son, then about twelve, asked, "Why would you even want to live if you can't move at all?" He didn't intend it as an unkind question. It was, rather, the result of hours of empathy, of trying to figure out what it felt like to be his mom.

How could I explain to him that participating in his growth and development, and that of his sister, was far more valuable and fulfilling to me than mere physical movement? I'm lucky that I was never an athlete or performer, and that movement itself was never an important goal in my life, unlike my athletic husband and my kids.

In March 2000, I had a feeding tube inserted, acknowledging that I could no longer obtain sufficient nutrition by mouth. Losing my ability to speak and swallow was at least as upsetting to me as losing the ability to move, because my ability to communicate, and thus my relationships, was directly affected.

People often ask about my spiritual development throughout this experience. I never was a very spiritual person, and I am not now. Any life-changing experience will cause some spiritual exploration, and mine was no different. One friend brought me a copy of *Why Bad Things Happen to Good People* by Rabbi Harold S. Kushner. Reading his work satisfied me that my illness was not an act of God, that it had occurred in spite of all God's good work, and that I could remain assured that God was on my side and would provide me with the strength I needed to deal with this new experience. I found that concept comforting, and I believe that strength is indeed provided in the form of the love and support of family and friends.

Another friend brought me some of the work of Thich Nhat Hanh, the Buddhist monk and teacher. Most of that material was on tape, and I listened to it in the hospital after my tracheotomy while I was adjusting to my new life of being on life support. It was very soothing and peaceful, and my pursuit of inner peace had already commenced with the simple act of listening to his words. I surprised myself as I absorbed his message. In spite of having had no Buddhist training or education, and in spite of my previously hectic and often heedless life, I had somehow developed the skills that Thich Nhat Hanh advocated. I found comfort again in the belief that I had the strength I needed to be at peace with my experience. Never had anger, hopelessness, or despair been part of my illness, whether by the grace of God, the love and support of those around me, exceptional medical treatment and care, or simply Prozac—or perhaps the combination of all of those factors. I feel very blessed to have been spared so much of the emotional anguish that often accompanies degenerative disease.

Yet another friend brought me Christopher Reeve's *Still Me*, which he wrote as soon after his accident as humanly possible. My daughter, then sixteen, lay with me for hours after my trach surgery, reading it to me and with me. Christopher and his wife Dana were terrific role models, and the account of his road toward recovery is very uplifting; it shows a man of tremendous spirit. I mused about the differences between becoming disabled through a traumatic injury and a degenerative disease. With the latter, there is no one to blame, unless one is of a mind to blame God. In the former, there are plenty of potential parties to blame: the horse, the course, the groundskeepers, the hat manufacturer, etc. But it was not in Christopher's nature to blame anyone, and he was able to move on and continue a very productive and fulfilling life.

Too often in my law practice, I saw anger and blame cripple victims as much as the physical injuries they incurred, preventing them from getting over it and moving on with their lives. "Getting over it" is a conscious choice. I believe people are either blessed with that immediate choice, like Christopher Reeve, or else they must learn it, which can be extremely difficult. In my case, I was blessed with circumstances in which there was no one to blame, and that in itself is a source of strength.

Life has changed dramatically for all of us since my diagnosis. At that time, I was still practicing law. Our family lived in Carlsbad, California, where my husband works; my children were in school, both in Del Mar, about twenty miles away. We eventually moved from our Carlsbad home to a little one-story house in Solana Beach where both of our children switched to local public schools because I was no longer able to chauffeur them long distances. Family vacations ceased and, instead, the kids took turns going on mini-vacations with cousins and friends, while Ron took occasional dive trips with friends.

Holiday celebrations came to rely more on the efforts of other people. Ron perfected his skills at barbecuing turkeys and planning potlucks, and my kids each contributed special recipes. I learned to accept that the table linens might not be ironed perfectly and the centerpieces might be less elaborate. Before my illness, I used to suffer the same tunnel vision we all get when our lives are too busy. Slowing down because of an illness reminds me that the presence of family and friends is the important thing in life. That reminder comes as a gift that compensates for our physical losses to varying degrees, depending on how much I choose to remain engaged in the important, valuable aspects of our lives.

I choose to remain fully engaged for three reasons. First, I am blessed with a disease that is relatively free of physical pain, so that it leaves my mind and energy relatively intact. Second, I am constantly reminded of the important people and events in my life, and of ways that I can make a difference. And third, I have wonderful, caring doctors and nurses who do everything possible to encourage and assist me in being as active and busy as possible.

I continue to attend my son's important events at school; go online to keep up with his assignments and testing schedules; and communicate with his guidance counselor, teachers, doctors, and friends' parents. When he was engaged in competitive sports, I attended his games and parent meetings, and participated in his carpools as best I could in my handicap-modified van with only three passenger seats. I buy his clothes and essentials; shop for his birthday and favorite healthy foods; and nag him to eat dinner, shower, and pick up his things. I am still the mean old mom, the disciplinarian who always seeks to impose structure and rules, but I also enjoy catching him doing things that are helpful, thoughtful, or otherwise special, and letting him know it. We don't spend as much time in direct communication as I would like, but then, who does with a seventeen-year-old son? He knows I love him and try to be fair, although sometimes he thinks fairness is just against my nature.

My daughter is a junior at Pomona College and is currently on a semester abroad in the Netherlands, my father's birthplace. I e-mail her almost every day, and in many ways, our relationship has been enriched since my illness. Our communication is almost telepathic. She can actually understand my words over the phone; she is the only person who can. I am a better listener now, but once in a while, I lapse into motherly advice. I try to let her know I feel good about her independence and her balance of freedom and responsibility. Right now, the most important growth for Sara is in feeling confident about her independent judgment and continuing to stay on track toward achieving her long-term goals. I feel I can best support those developments the same way as any other parent does—with verbal encouragement and evidence of my absolute love and support.

Although I am physically unable to be a complete wife, I try to improve as a spouse in other ways. Listening skills have certainly helped. I used to be so overextended and unsure of my effectiveness in juggling the roles of lawyer, parent, wife, daughter, sister, and friend. I needed a lot of reassurance from all sources. Now that I feel free of those self-imposed expectations, I can relax and give—instead of take—reassurance, encouragement, and support. Whereas I used to resent time that Ron spent in the lone pursuit of scuba diving, I now encourage it and share his joy of conquest when he brings home lobsters or fish. I even enjoy his sense of humor that used to drive me crazy. As with everything, I used to be impatient with him when he wanted to relax and enjoy the moment. In this ultimate test of love and devotion, Ron's patience, love, and dedication prove a tremendous source of strength for me.

My mother and I have always had a lot of traditional mother-daughter baggage. One of my biggest concerns at the onset of my disease was hiding my physical condition from her. But the disease progressed so rapidly that it was clearly impossible. I remembered my relief at the outcome of my tests, knowing that my disease was not hereditary and that my children would be spared. But my mother was not as lucky; this was happening to one of her children. I was surprised and impressed with my mother's overt reaction to my diagnosis: She was all business. She immediately arranged for household help so that I could remain in charge of the household as much as possible. I guess we think alike more than I had realized.

My sister Rikki has made me feel like I am no longer the demanding little sister. Rikki is the only person I know who would get all dressed up to take her final exams in college. While everyone else was in sweats or unchanged from the day before, Rikki was always fresh as a daisy. She had this theory that if she looked well, she felt well, and if she felt well, she would do good work. Simple logic. So from the beginning of my disease, Rikki has taken charge of my wardrobe, stocking it with designer clothes and accessories. Her theory works. Never am I tempted to stay in bed, do nothing, or succumb to depression. And although I occasionally sneak out to Ross or Marshalls for less-polished garb, I never, *ever* wear sweats!

I lost my father to Parkinson's disease when I was twenty-one and had just finished college. He was eighty at that time, and he made the choice not to continue treatment while this degenerative neurological disease sapped the rest of his strength and resolve. My father had suffered terribly during World War II, when he lost much of his family in Holland during the Holocaust. But he also had a tremendous ability for rejuvenation and a natural joy and love of life. I could not judge the choice my father made at a late and dark time in his life, when he felt that all his work on earth was finished. But I have no doubt that his choice affected my choice at a very different stage in my life, when my children were young and still had so much to learn. Choosing a ventilator—choosing life on life support—was not a difficult choice at that time, and I believe that my knowledge of what my father had endured before I was even born, and his strength and resolve, made my choice the natural one for me.

Friends near and far have been incredibly loving and supportive. Shortly after we moved out of our Carlsbad house, when my hands had weakened to the point where I was unable to hold a knife to make a sandwich, one of my local friends divinely intervened and organized a cooking roster. That was about six years ago. The same dozen or so friends have been nurturing my family and me, body and soul, ever since. Old high school, college, and law school friends keep in touch with e-mails and visits and encourage my writing. And of course there is my book club, my rock. We started about ten years ago, well before any of us suspected that one of us would suffer a catastrophic illness and become so dependent on all the others. I try to continue to participate in book discussions by writing out my thoughts and reactions to each book and sharing at our meetings. A few times a year, I organize luncheons to bring my friends together. I usually start collecting things in summer to put together holiday baskets for all my cooking-roster friends.

Several years ago, when my insurance case manager and I discussed how long I would be likely to carry on, my flippant response was, "As long as I can engage in my favorite two activities: eating and talking." I still enjoy the taste of coffee and chocolate in the morning, although I glean precious little nutrition from them. And I still orally communicate occasional, directional, word-like sounds to my family and my nurses. What I do certainly doesn't qualify as eating or talking. But, as Christopher Reeve pointed out in *Still Me*, we can't know whether or how we will tolerate and adapt to new circumstances and challenges until we actually face them. In my experience, the biggest changes of all, besides the obvious physical change, were my recognition of and focus on what was truly important to me: the people I love and carrying on relationships with them.

If I can only do that through writing, so be it. I have just broken through another tolerance barrier in the course of my disease.

Fear:
A Path to Courage

Marcelline Burns

Some things cannot be spoken or discovered until we have been stuck, incapacitated, or blown off course for awhile. Plain sailing is pleasant, but you are not going to explore many unknown realms that way.

—DAVID WHYTE,
*The Heart Aroused: Poetry and the
Preservation of the Soul in Corporate America*

On a sun-drenched summer afternoon, a small boat marina in Southern California buzzes with activity. The main channel is astir with boats, small and large, sail and power. The occasional whiff of diesel fumes only slightly mars the beauty of the blue water and the white sails.

A youngster in a sailing dinghy hasn't quite learned how to cope with shifting winds and sails dangerously into the path of a larger vessel. The reckless skipper of a spanking-new sloop tacks back and forth across steady traffic in the main channel, steadfastly ignoring the boaters who must maneuver abruptly to avoid him. Chaotic? At times, yes. Yet those of us who thrive in a world of water generally escape disaster despite the violations of rights-of-way. And we suffer our humiliation quietly when it is we who err.

Returning from a recent spirit-renewing afternoon on the ocean as a guest on a friend's powerboat, it was my pleasure to watch a young woman of abundant skill and grace. Typically, a man is the skipper of a pleasure boat, and the women aboard are crew or passengers. This young woman, however, was alone as she sailed a midsize sloop through the late afternoon congestion. We paralleled her as she made way down the main channel, and I was able to watch not only how she handled her boat, but also, importantly, how she handled herself. Young, suntanned, blonde, attractive. . . . In appearance, she was everything that the label "Southern California girl" brings to mind, but she was uniquely more, much more. She was smiling slightly. She did not appear unfriendly, but she did seem uninterested in much of the activity all around her. She was focused, never frantic, as she tacked and adjusted sails to maneuver into a finger, and then expertly into a slip. She dropped the jib at just the right moment, and as the boat slowed, she calmly stepped onto the dock with a line. Perfect!

I applauded her silently, "You go, girl!"

As we motored to a slip in the next finger, I lost sight of her, but her image lingered in my mind's eye. Much later that night, as I lay in my bed courting sleep and staring into darkness, I thought about her unusual display of confidence and courage. Sailing alone in the Pacific Ocean, even on a sunny day with moderate breezes, is not an activity for the fainthearted. Westerly winds can (and do) blow up suddenly with unexpected ferocity. To capably handle both the sails and the tiller is the mark of skill and experience. Even so, things can go wrong. The ocean is notoriously unforgiving, and one bad decision may be followed quickly by mounting crises. Happily, it occurs only rarely, but seasoned sailors with ample crew sometimes encounter unexpected weather or equipment problems that get them into serious trouble. This very young woman, who serenely handled her boat like an old timer, had a very good day . . . all by herself. I wish that I could tell her that seeing her made my already-good day even better.

Why do I tell you this story about a young woman who remains a stranger to me? I tell you, because it has to do with courage: how we find courage, or how we fail to find it. It has to do with confronting the darkness of fear, and to talk about that, I need to tell you yet another sailing story. It happened a very long time ago, and it was a sentinel event in my life.

It was the Fourth of July holiday in that now-distant year. We had four days of freedom from our everyday responsibilities. The weather was perfect. Our ketch was ready, and we made a happy start for a trip to the islands with non-sailor friends aboard. The friends had been college classmates, and we reveled in the unusual opportunity to spend time with them. The fact that they had never been aboard a sailing vessel did not concern any of us. My husband and I sailed almost every weekend, and the ketch rigging made it easy for the two of us to handle our boat. Always, he was the skipper and I was his first mate, and we had years of experience sailing this boat and others before it.

Because the day was picture perfect, we chose a route to the east and south of a small island, planning then to cross the channel to a bigger island and a safe anchorage by early to mid-afternoon. It was a small adventure, not our regular practice, and thus we had not anticipated how drastically the wind would drop on the sheltered side. Because we used auxiliary power only reluctantly, we first sought to keep moving by going away from the lee of the island. We adjusted sails. We told each other, "The wind is sure to pick up soon." Later, much too late as it turned out, we capitulated and began to motor toward our destination. We had been right! The wind picked up. Once out of the shadow of the island, we were in gale-force winds. When the anemometer pinned at its maximum, I understood that we had a problem.

Even with the engine at full throttle, we made

little progress. For the first time ever, we took green water over the bow of our sturdy vessel as we ploughed through confused seas. Four hours passed, and the sun had set before the difficult passage ended. We arrived at the anchorage only to find that a large holiday crowd had arrived before we did. Dozens of vessels were already anchored, and the sheltered cove was filled to capacity. The magnitude of our problem suddenly took a giant leap.

There were no other safe anchorages. We would have to anchor even though we would be far out in the channel. The hook went down, and our anxious watch began. Within minutes we knew the anchor had not held. We were dragging. Try again. Drag again. Try again. Drag again. It was no use. We were in deep water, and the anchor chain was not long enough. Sometime during the anchoring attempts, fear first reared its ugly head. I tasted bitter bile, and my heart thudded uncomfortably. I didn't know it yet, but I would be much more frightened before the night was over.

To this day, I cannot fully explain all of the events of that night. Although what happened next remains beyond my understanding, I now accept it without judgment. Furthermore, I believe that a purpose played out during the long, black hours. That purpose pulled me through a wall of fear to the salvation of courage.

First, without a word, our friends went below. Since leaving deck to check on them was not an option for me for the rest of the night, I don't know whether they climbed into their bunks and went to sleep or huddled together in frightened misery. We never discussed it, and they never sailed with us again.

Then, the unthinkable! My husband, the skipper, abandoned his duties. I would not have believed it possible, but the nausea that had been plaguing him for several hours escalated, probably because he, too, was frightened. He wiped his face after heaving into the black waters and very calmly said, "Put the damn boat on the rocks for all I care." Then he, too, disappeared below.

Stunned as I was at that moment, I realized that having never been subject to motion sickness, it was not possible for me to assess its miseries with fairness. In any case, there was no time to think about it. I was as alone as I'd ever been during my entire life. Horrific fear engulfed me. The wind was howling. We were twenty-five nautical miles from the mainland. I had never sailed this boat, or any boat, alone. Yet here I was, utterly on my own, and it was survival time.

I had always been afraid of many things: afraid of being hurt, afraid of failing, afraid of rejection . . . truth be told, I was tiptoeing through life. Fears had marked my days, beginning, I think, when my parent's raging quarrels threatened my child's small world and I hid in a closet to shut out their angry voices. It grew when I was pushed ahead in school into classes with older, bigger children, and when I was the new kid in school as we moved and moved again. Poorly dressed, cross-eyed, and with a face full of freckles, I surely was not a child who attracted affection and comfort from either children or adults. Clumsy and shy, I was an easy target for teases and bullies.

Until that July night, my responses to fear-arousing situations and people were avoidance and accommodation. Run away. Don't compete. Don't try for the special privilege. Be nice. Smile. Make good grades. Agree. Maybe no one will notice. Confront? Challenge? Resist? Not me. I did well in school, married young, and until that July night, I continued to avoid and adapt.

Did a rush of adrenaline push me to action? Perhaps it was a guardian angel. Whatever the source, the fear that paralyzed me slowly lessened a little. I understood that whether the boat and the people aboard would survive depended on me. What could I do?

Analytical skills seem to be my birthright, and they served me well as I weighed the options. There really were only three. One, I could try again to anchor. That option was rejected, because I reckoned that my single-handed efforts would be futile. Two, it might be possible to simply motor back and forth in the wind shadow of the big island until daybreak, when the wind velocity would drop. Would there be enough fuel for eight or more hours? Would I be able to stay awake and alert, peering into darkness hour after hour? Staying out of the wind would mean running close to shore; what if the engine failed? That option went down in face of the risks.

The third and only other option . . . go home.

Was that a reasonable choice? While still in sheltered waters, I could put up the jib, and that would be enough sail in the gale conditions. But could I handle the boat when the full force of the wind struck? Maybe. It was a full keel vessel. I had been at the helm in twenty-knot winds on many occasions. There was no other reasonable option. I would do it.

I raised the jib and motored into the open ocean. As I turned off the engine and braced myself, the wheel spun under my hand and the boat heeled sharply. The wind was the strongest and the waves were the biggest I'd ever encountered. My arms were not strong enough to steer, and we plunged into the darkness on a course that was not of my choosing. By the compass glowing red in the darkness, I saw that our heading would take us far off course for the marina. That problem, however, could be deferred. First, there would be hours of being buffeted, listening to the boat's ominous creaks and groans.

Gradually, as the hours dragged by, I began to believe that we might make it. Despite the mountainous seas, none of the waves broke on deck, and mercifully I remained dry. Holding the course as steady as possible, I relaxed ever so slightly, looked up and about, and realized that the wind had cleared the skies. There were multitudes of brilliantly spectacular stars. I was alone and frightened in a world of magical beauty.

One, then two hours passed, with the boat rising on monstrous wave after monstrous wave, then hurtling off the crests into their troughs. Slowly, slowly we moved onward without disaster. Midway across the channel, the wind began to slacken, the seas flattened a bit, and onshore lights came into view. A clear vision arose in my mind's eye of families safely sleeping in their homes. Only a matter of miles separated me from them, but as they slept, I faced down demons, both real and metaphorical.

The hours ticked by. As we came nearer to the mainland, the wind almost completely died and the ocean calmed. I corrected our heading, and sailed into the main channel. How strange! No boats were moving, and there were no cars on the streets at this late hour. The only sound was the soft swish of our wake as we moved through the mirror-like water. The danger was over, and we were safely home.

Several decades have elapsed. My beloved husband became lost in the mindlessness of Alzheimer's disease and died. The ketch, too, is gone. I like to think that someone still sails it to wondrous places, building a storehouse of memories of good times as we did when it belonged to us. Among my treasures is a vivid memory of that Fourth of July, which changed me forever. It enabled me to confront fear and move forever out of its shadow. Oh, challenges and tests abound, day after day and year after year, but the courage gained on that night supports me, and I am able to face them head-on. I cope from strength instead of fear with whatever hand life deals me.

I no longer tremble at the thought that life is filled with risk. I accept that my body and ego are fragile. I realize that not every challenge is worthy. I know that foolish bravado gains nothing. I also know that the fear conquered during a frightful night illuminated a new pathway to courage. There is beauty in the darkest of times.

Finding My Soul's Path

Lauren Artress

All of the larger-than-life questions about our presence here on earth and what gifts we have to offer are spiritual questions. To seek answers to these questions is to seek a sacred path.

—*Walking a Sacred Path*

I t is probably an understatement to say I was "bitten by the labyrinth." I didn't have a mountaintop experience that particular evening, when I first walked a labyrinth. Instead, surprisingly, the labyrinth kept on working with me long after I stepped out of it.

About one month after my initial walk, I began to feel that the hound of heaven was hunting me down. It was getting closer and closer, but each time I would turn around, it vanished so I could not engage it with my naked eye. After about three months, a rest-less frustration was taking over my life. Out of pure desperation, I found myself walking in a circle in my living room, yelling to some unknown force, "What is it? What is it?" Finally my frustration peaked and I yelled at the top of my lungs, "WHAT IS IT?!"

The answer came in a clear, simple thought: "Put the labyrinth in the cathedral."

"Who me?" I thought. Then I remembered that I worked for a large cathedral, and my ministry was to address the spiritual hunger in this country by build-ing a bridge of understanding between the traditional church and the non-traditional forms of spirituality that are springing up in our culture. I already had some-what of a track record of doing new and interesting spiritual programs, but why on earth put a labyrinth in Grace Cathedral? However, I had my orders and I set about on this task—reading books, meeting just the right person to further my education, and planning a trip to Our Lady of Chartres Cathedral in France, one of the holiest places on the planet and dedicated to the Sacred Feminine, to do further on-site research. I can't say I knew what I was doing except following the en-ergy, so to speak, that invisibly guided me.

Over the years, I have found this type of guid-ance to be true for many intuitive creators. In fact, I found an anonymous quote that describes this "mole under the ground" kind of creativity: "Please excuse the inefficiency of my work. The nature of it requires such a high degree of complexity that I simply don't know what I am doing!" I was following an invisible map and only a little of the vision was clear to me. I could imagine many people walking together prayerfully, meditatively on a circuitous path lit by candlelight, finding their center. And with that vision came the unfolding of my own circuitous path, which resulted in finding my soul assignment.

In 1986, I had received an invitation to serve as canon pastor, a senior position, at Grace Cathedral in San Francisco. I was settled in my life. I owned a lovely lake house in northern New Jersey and commuted to New York City four days a week, leaving me leisurely three-day weekends with my partner and lots of time for friendship, fun, and rest. However, while I had a thriving psychotherapy practice in Manhattan and loved this work, I had an intuitive sense that I was not yet connected to my soul assignment. I was not doing all that I was here on earth to do.

After receiving the invitation, I drew inward to reflect and evaluate whether this was the right move to make. It was a time of expansion, and what I gained from my reflection was support and encouragement that something important would manifest out of my work in San Francisco.

I had many strengths in pastoral ministry and loved teamwork. The cathedral offered numerous opportunities for both. However, my work in a church—

let alone a cathedral—was limited and I was not a strong administrator. Because of these gaps in my experience, I knew that Grace Cathedral was going to be a "boot camp." It would be an intense setting to develop both basic and advanced skills, and to challenge me spiritually in unique ways.

Some women learn leadership skills gradually, over time, through experiences that build upon one another. Others of us learn by being shoved into situations. That was what happened to me. The first two years felt like I was on a long toboggan ride down a snowy mountain without brakes. I had no time to make up excuses or feel sorry for myself.

Initially, I had to develop skills in two major areas: preaching and officiating at the Choral Eucharist. Both were new to me, although I had more experience preaching than I did with singing in public. After my first-ever preaching experience in college, I received a one-sentence critique: "Lauren's sermon was a series of disconnected thoughts." I had my work cut out for me.

Two weeks after I arrived in San Francisco, I was assigned to preach at the main service to about seven hundred congregants. The very first time I was in the high pulpit—which is forty-five feet from the first pew—I was so intimidated I could hardly open my mouth. When testing the microphone and sound system—to learn to manage a seven-second delay—all I could say was, "Testing, testing, one, two, three. . . ." I couldn't rehearse my sermon because I was too frightened to speak in front of the sound technician!

Many newfound friends cheered me on before the sermon, but few spoke to me afterward. My message was much more advanced than my skill in delivering it, compounded with handling the voice delay. Most challenging was the sensitive material assigned that day; this text dealing with Sodom and Gomorrah came up in the lectionary right after a brutal hate crime and the Supreme Court of Georgia ruling that drew national attention and reinforced archaic homophobic laws. I was in raw pain for days after I preached. I remember taking long walks to console myself. Even then, walking was healing to me because my mind would quiet down and I would feel at peace. Eventually, I concluded that if I had made the wrong choice in coming to the cathedral, I would have the strength to recognize it and break my contract. After a few redeeming sermons, however, things began to feel more comfortable. This experience helped me find the grit inside of me to continue to speak my mind. However, I needed to learn the skills and sensitivities to do so: nuance, humor, and humility, for starters.

Grace Cathedral is a rather intimidating place to do anything solo, but preaching from the high pulpit was easier than singing when officiating at the service. I was far more intimidated to chant the Choral Eucharist than I was to preach. Although I had never sung a note in public, I had to lead the congregation in sung worship. When I stood up in front of the congregation to chant, I sounded like a frightened chicken about to get its head cut off. People were embarrassed for me and couldn't look me straight in the eye. I was too numb to be mortified, though as I thawed out, I filled up with pain, embarrassment, and dread since I had to do it again.

The cantor from the cathedral's music department stepped in to help; we started voice lessons. He insisted that I sing in a soprano range, though I am naturally an alto. These lessons were painful and though they continued, I failed to improve. I could feel people shrink away from me on the mornings I had to officiate the main service. My lack of skill was so troubling that after a few months, I was quietly dropped from the schedule. Finally, the dean suggested I get private voice lessons from one of the congregation members. The first question she asked me was why I was not singing in my natural voice! From that day on, I began to use my natural range in chanting.

Since my comfort level in the pulpit was much higher than singing the service, I decided to risk chanting during a sermon, which freed me considerably. It also let the congregation know that I had a decent voice, a fact that was impossible to discern earlier.

After a period of helpful voice lessons and a rest from officiating the Choral Eucharist, it was time to step forward again to chant the service. I was very nervous the night before. And I wasn't feeling serene during the elegant, solemn procession down the long center aisle and around the altar. I knew that once I reached my prayer desk, I would have to sing, "Blessed be the one, holy, and living God." I was frightened the words wouldn't come out of my mouth.

As I raised my arms in the priestly Orans position and opened my mouth to sing, I felt like a frozen robin perched upon a telephone wire on an icy winter morning. I was a frightened woman who had no choice but to open her mouth and trust: Trust the work I had done to prepare for this moment, trust my strength, and trust that whatever came out was a beginning that I could adjust and work with as I moved further into the chant.

And that is what I did. To my surprise, out came a measured, solid note, and I knew I had found my voice. In that moment, my initiation was complete.

Slowly, the wind shifted to come 'round my back, and my soul assignment began to unfold directly. In discovering the mystical qualities of the labyrinth, I also had found the answer to my unproductive sitting practice that failed me in stressful moments, just when I needed it most. By moving my body, I found that I could discharge all the pent-up mental energy that I expend in thinking. The labyrinth could offer me peaceful, quiet relief.

I knew I needed to learn much more about labyrinths before we could create one at Grace Cathedral, so I made arrangements to visit the labyrinth in Chartres Cathedral. Through a stroke of synchronicity, five other people from the congregation were traveling to France at the same time, so we arranged to meet. Although we tried to get permission to move the hundreds of chairs that cover the eight-hundred-year-old inlaid labyrinth, we wound up moving them ourselves—without official permission—to discover the treasure hidden underneath. The labyrinth itself felt light and happy. We felt a joy in the air when we walked it, as if someone had thrown handfuls of stardust in the air! Truly a golden moment. . . .

> M*y first glimpse of Chartres Cathedral remains a distinct memory. It stands majestically on a hilltop among miles of wheat fields. At a distance there is no hint of a city that lies below its awesome presence. The cathedral was built on the highest sacred ground available, most likely following a long line of spiritual traditions. . . . Looking back on that experience, I feel we had touched the Holy Spirit. Each of us had ventured to the center of our beings in the Chartres Labyrinth that day. I received the embrace of Mary. I had, unknown to me at the time, ventured into her glorious web.*
> —Walking a Sacred Path

Back at Grace Cathedral, many people gathered to help sew, draw, and paint the first canvas labyrinth that is still in use today. We opened this labyrinth in December 1991, during the twenty-four-hour New

Year's Eve singing event. The line waiting to walk the labyrinth lasted six hours! We opened it to the public regularly and, as word of mouth spread, we needed to expand the hours the labyrinth was open. The demand was so great that we commissioned a wool carpet—the tapestry labyrinth—to be available during open cathedral hours.

In 1995, we dedicated the Melvin E. Swig Memorial Labyrinth and Meditation Garden near the entrance to the cathedral. This outdoor terrazzo stone labyrinth is open twenty-four hours a day. I know from the stories I receive via e-mail that it is used throughout the wee hours of the morning, as well as in the bright light of day.

Now, after thirteen years, the floor tapestry labyrinth has been removed and placed in storage to eventually become the centerpiece of the new retreat center at Veriditas, a not-for-profit created in 1995 to "pepper the planet" with labyrinths and to facilitate the transformation of the human spirit. In its place is the first inlaid limestone and marble labyrinth found in the nave of a cathedral in several hundred years.

Today there are more than 3,500 labyrinths in the United States alone—in prisons, public schools, college campuses, churches, hospitals and healing centers, memorial parks, retreat centers, and cathedrals. And the labyrinth movement is taking root and flowering throughout the world, quickly becoming an accepted spiritual practice for those of us with unruly minds and a desire to open our hearts.

My soul assignment was far beyond my wildest imaginings, so it took time to saturate my consciousness and become clear to me: I am called to work with a sacred pattern replicated from the floor of Chartres Cathedral. Through the simple act of walking the single, but circuitous, path—alone or in large numbers—the mind can quiet and the heart can open. It changes lives by helping people find their center, their grounded nature. The labyrinth speaks to all faith traditions because the metaphor of the path is universal. It connects us to embodied wisdom and supports our pilgrimage through this earthly life. It provides a portal to a participatory experience of the symbolic world. In that world, the path becomes a larger metaphor of the Path of Life that—whether we are conscious of it or not—we are all walking together.

Before the opening of the canvas labyrinth in 1991, a reporter from the *San Francisco Chronicle* came to interview people who walked its path. Following the interview, I had several anxious, tumultuous days. Out of my fear and discomfort, I called to ask him not to print the article because I truly did not feel I had a grasp of what I was doing. But he said, "It's too late. The article will be published on December 19."

I remember waking up in fear that Friday morning. I trembled when I opened the paper. Instantly I saw a lovely photograph of our freshly painted canvas, and the caption read: "The Path to Enlightenment." My immediate thought was, "Ah, so *that's* what we're doing. Yes, I'll certainly sign up for that!"

Sliding Glass Door

Janet Grace Riehl

*What a beautiful and what a healing mystery it is that
from contemplating, continually and fearlessly, the truth
of change and impermanence, we come slowly to find
ourselves face to face, in gratitude and joy, with the truth
of the changeless, with the truth of the deathless, unending
nature of mind!*

—SOGYAL RINPOCHE,
The Tibetan Book of Living and Dying

We met because I crashed into a sliding glass door.

I'd taken off my glasses to have my face painted at a friend's fortieth birthday party. Pastel bands of face paint matched my costume, and because wearing glasses spoiled the festive look, I tucked them into my pocket. And then crashed into the glass door.

I'd seen the door open only a minute before. But as I walked forward to go into the living room, my face made full contact with the glass pane—whack!—and bounced off. I stood there, stunned as a bird might who suddenly encounters glass instead of yielding air. Same whack. Same stun.

Embarrassed at my awkwardness, I did my best to become invisible. But witnesses had heard the whack and seen the impact. There was no way I was going to get out of this without huge helpings of solicitude.

"Oh, my dear!" "Sit down here," "Would you like a glass of water?" came the cries of alarm and helpfulness. My embarrassment deepened.

Sitting on the Louis XIV armchair in the entryway, I recovered enough to know that I wasn't thinking straight and would benefit from the offered pampering. I allowed myself to be propped up on pillows on a plump velvet couch. A china cup of Earl Grey tea appeared on a silver tray. Well-wishers and caretakers multiplied around my makeshift throne as news of the mishap percolated through the party. Like it or not, I was receiving callers.

The theme of the birthday party was "Kids Again," with each guest in costume and contributing a favorite childhood game or prop. My prop was a joke book from the 1950s that I'd found in a thrift store. As the pampering took hold, I reveled in this rare opportunity to hold court. One of my courtiers held my hand, stroked my forehead, and spoke soothingly. Feeling nurtured, I roused myself enough to ask his name. "Jerry," he said.

With a painted canary singing in a birdcage on his cheek, Jerry perched on an ottoman, his crutches neatly stacked next to the couch. Jerry read horrible jokes out of the joke book until I laughed myself silly. Fortified by all that oxygen, I sat up. My court, satisfied that I was ok, drifted away.

All but Jerry. He stayed, and our thirteen-year friendship began: Thirteen roller-coaster years that brought us into each other's inner circles and qualified us as long-term friends. The first five years, we dated on and off. We lived together a few months, decided not to marry, and ended our courtship as a romantic couple. The last eight, we simply loved each other without too much fuss. That hard-earned intimacy buoyed us through heartbreaks in love affairs with others, money and legal crises, major surgeries, Jerry's journey from crutches to wheelchair, business decisions, work collaborations, my graduation from art school, and relocation from the Bay Area around San Francisco to a rural area in Northern California.

But what our friendship couldn't withstand was the arrival of his dream girl, Brenda, who fulfilled the fortune-cookie promise that Jerry posted in the corner of his kitchen cabinet: "Your dream of home and family will come true."

Out of respect for the new woman in his life, we

rarely contacted each other after they met. But when my mother told me she wasn't bathing because of her fear of falling in the tub, I remembered a bath bench Jerry had used and called him. After he graciously gave me the information I needed, he said, "Brenda and I are getting married next month. We wanted to have the wedding while my mother can still enjoy it. I'm sorry you and I haven't been as close since Brenda's been in my life."

Did this mean, "Good-bye, Janet. I'm sorry I won't be able to invite you to my wedding"? I hoped not. But during the weeks approaching the wedding, no invitation arrived. When the date for the wedding had come and gone, I called.

"Did someone tell the zebra joke?" I asked. Jerry's father had told this slightly naughty and sexy joke at family gatherings throughout his life, much to his wife's chagrin. After his father's death, Jerry continued to tell it.

"Yes, my brother told the joke, but he got it backwards. I had to tell it, finally."

For years, I'd been Jerry's confidant and cheerleader in his pursuit of a woman who would love and accept him fully, including his physical disability, and share his life. I wished I'd been there to hear the joke, and celebrate this longed-for moment with him. Why hadn't that been possible?

I finally bore down on my pride and asked him this question. They had decided they'd be uncomfortable if a woman he'd previously been intimate with attended the wedding. That was his answer.

I'd crashed into another sliding glass door. Same whack. Same stun. Losing one of the few people in my life who held the thread of my personal history scared me. While new friends aren't hard to come by, maturing an old friendship takes time. In a society where even committed relationships frequently crash, the number of people with whom we can share memories, jokes, stories, and growth shrinks. The ground you share can shift—whether through death, distance, quarrels, or marriage. Every time I moved or made a major change in my life, a layer of friendships sloughed away like slipping out of a skin.

I asked my father, then eighty-five, for his wisdom. My father knew Jerry. In an old photo, Jerry is sitting atop our ancient tractor during a visit to our homeplace one summer. He's giving a city-slicker wave to Pop, the old-man-of-the-mountain. My father is a self-taught folk treasure and one of the strongest men I've even known.

"I can offer you sympathy and understanding for the loss you feel," he told me. "There's a French phrase I learned in World War II that translates, 'So goes the war.' But the meaning is much richer, more like 'Such are the fortunes of war. Because these misfortunes are unavoidable, we must handle them the best we can.'

"Jerry did exactly the right thing for his new relationship," my father told me. "Yet, even when the wedding is happy from the standpoint of the two getting married, that doesn't prevent unhappy side results for other people. A line from one of my poems says, 'We live and love, meet and part, and broken hearts must pay.' Losing friends along the way is one of life's little deaths."

Then my father sang a snatch of a song from the early 1900s: "Wedding Bells Are Breaking Up (That Old Gang of Mine)," by Sammy Fain and Irving Kahal:

> *There goes Jack, there goes Jim*
> *Down to Lover's Lane*
> *Now and then we meet again*
> *But they don't seem the same*
> *Gee, I get that lonesome feeling*
> *When I hear the church bells chime*
> *Those wedding bells are breaking up*
> *That old gang of mine*

He told me stories of how he'd lost old pals once they, too, found their dream girls, just as Jerry had.

My last act of friendship to Jerry is to let go. Letting go is much harder than hanging on through tough times. I will miss you in my life, Jerry. May your marriage be long and happy. May you grow old in the company and comfort of your bride.

As for myself, may I have the strength to believe that no heart breaks in vain, to believe that our hearts must break—are designed to break—in order to widen their embrace. May my heart mend, scar, and break again and again—until I understand how vast the heart-mind really is.

FIVE

Divine Interventions

Wisdom looks to see the jewel or flower shining beyond unexpected places or secure positions.

—A SPANISH SAYING

You live among the stars,
there are flowers at your feet,
and everyone you meet is God
with another face.

Surrounded by the beautiful reminders of God's love in nature, we also meet the divine in people who surprise and amaze us with their generosity and love. They persuade us that we are protected and treasured by the same invisible life force that uplifts the earth and finds worth in all creations.

Timeless stories by heroines who are spiritual optimists teach us how to respond to our own divine promptings to go beyond pain and limitations to find truth, relationships, and integrity. Friends, strangers, and unseen forces intervene in times of need, responsibility, and joy. They awaken us and we see again with fresh sharp eyes and revelations. Their arrivals signal that it is time to let go of what needs to be sacrificed and to hold on to what needs to be balanced and restored.

Each story takes us to a different world of possibilities. Each is filled with grace, devotion, and intuition by women who inspire us to give ourselves completely. Each woman convinces us that nothing can conquer our spirits, and her story will live on as a link between the human and the divine.

Premonitions, Dreams, and Whispers

Jennifer Thompson Trepanier

I slept and dreamt that life was joy. I awoke and saw that life was service. I acted and behold, service was joy.
—RABINDRANATH TAGORE,
Rabindranath Tagore: An Anthology

She came as a whisper in the night. She tantalized me with her beauty. Visions of colorful saris streamed past my eyes. The warm and dusty air mingled with spices and transported me to another world as I walked streets filled with hundreds of people. I was in India.

It was the fourteenth night in a row that India

came to me in a dream. I longed to go there. My dreams
were calling me and guiding me there.

The next six months gracefully unfolded as everything fell into place. I was laid off from my job right
before I was going to give notice. Thanks to the generosity of a friend, I was able to live rent-free so that I
could save money for my journey.

When I walked the streets around my home in
San Francisco, I would get flashes of images of Indian
streets. I was entering an alternate reality. I could feel
her and see her in my dreams and my waking life. I was
creating my world . . . with intentions and visions.

Another dream came, this time of a remarkable
structure at sunset. I could see an enormous temple—
one of the most magnificent ones I had ever seen. It sat
abreast of what looked like a lake. I knew that if it was
real, I must go there. A week later, I flipped through
a magazine and there it was: Angkor Wat, the temple
in my dreams. I made plans to visit Cambodia where
I would walk into this glorious structure and then go
on to India.

I wanted to spend six months in Asia, but I had
no idea whether that was possible. The experiences I
had with my greatest teacher, a very rare autoimmune
disease that began when I was twelve, taught me to
have a positive perspective toward challenges in my
life. This illness brought me to the brink of death. I was
unable to get out of bed on my own. My body attacked
muscles, leaving me extremely weak and in extreme
pain. While helpless and relying on others to sustain

me physically as they carried me up stairs and helped me in and out of bed, spiritually I was strengthening and becoming deeply tuned in to the flow of my inner wisdom. I learned at twelve that it was important to let go of all expectations, for the body can fail—but Spirit never will. I learned to trust and be open, even in the midst of pain, and to place my focus on the gifts that were always coming my way. This wisdom would serve a whole new purpose in my life when the tsunami hit Asia on December 26, 2004.

Family and friends shared concerns about my health. How could someone whose immune system was already out of balance go to one of the filthiest places on earth? When I told them that I had had premonitions that there would be a lot of suffering and I knew I was meant to go, they grew even more concerned. I stayed up late and looked through the *Lonely Planet India* edition. I tried to picture what it would be like to go to another land so very different from mine. I would get tingles of excitement, as well as fear. I heard horror stories of people getting so sick and even dying from the unsanitary conditions. Although that caused some fear within me, I had a constant inner knowing that I must go.

"You don't have to go to another country for suffering. It's here in San Francisco," a friend pointed out. But the deep knowing in my soul said I would be OK. I had learned from my health struggles to listen to my intuition and to face my fears head-on, and that was what I was about to do.

My parents walked me into LAX. I looked into their eyes not knowing what was about to become of me. Would I survive the trip? Would I fail and have to come back to the States before my six-month journey was up? My mom's and stepfather's eyes welled up with tears as I waved goodbye. Walking to my gate, I felt a surge of strength and adventure like I had never felt before. I was embarking upon a journey far more powerful than I would ever know.

After a twenty-five-hour trek, I landed in Bangkok. I stepped outside and was hit with steamy, dense air. It was December 2 and about ninety-five degrees with dense humidity. I was a minority for the first time . . . and loving it. Thailand was beautiful, but I was eager to set foot in the temples of my dreams, and soon ventured by boat and bus to Cambodia.

My bus broke down twice in Cambodia. While many of the tourists just sat on the bus, I enjoyed the opportunity to get out and visit with the locals. The roads were dusty and dry—no pavement for miles and miles. I was greeted with smiles. The people were dressed in modest clothing and were eager to sell their handmade goods. Children with limbs stolen by hidden land mines and adults deformed by pesticides approached me to ask for money. I was made aware of how precious life is. The suffering and poverty were something I had never seen. It made me think of home in California where so many people worry about how they look or the status of their car, in contrast to people hoping to get their next meal or simply survive with missing limbs. I recognized that my perceptions of what is challenging and frustrating were now changed forever. Despite the desperate circumstances and conditions, I was in awe of the genuine beauty and kindness of the Cambodian people that radiated beyond their horrendous losses.

The next day, I walked through Angkor Wat. I was astounded. The temples, built between the eighth and sixteenth centuries, made me feel as if I had fallen into a never-ending story. This was a magical place where all ancient religions melted into magnificent temples immersed in forty miles of mystical forest. When I walked through this land, I could feel the ancestors from generations before watching over me. At a temple called the Bayon, one-hundred-foot stone heads watched visitors walk beneath them. I was in the presence of Stone Gods. It was eerie to feel the stone eyes look down upon me. I felt their power.

After leaving each temple, I was mobbed by kids selling souvenirs or begging for money. I embraced the duality of light and dark, rich and poor, sickness and health. I was awakening to the beauty in the simple life and realized how little I needed to be happy.

On my way to India, I was waiting to board the sky train when the ground began to shake.

I looked at another traveler. "Did you feel that?" I asked.

"No," he answered.

The earth beneath me moved slightly, but the small shifting I felt was being created by the world's most destructive tsunami.

Later I learned that more then 20,000 people were dead, and others were frightened that this was only the beginning. I was booked to fly into Chennai, in southern India, near the devastated area. I had to quickly decide whether to change my ticket to land in Delhi, far from the destruction, or go on as planned. I sat quietly with myself and felt that inner knowing: This was why I was in India. I was here to help.

Waiting in the airport, I watched CNN and saw the harsh images of the tsunami's destruction. The images were intense—women were screaming and crying for the loss of their families. The strength of Mother Nature to wipe out so many people was beyond my comprehension. I was eager to be a part of the relief effort rather than a voyeur on a couch. I was anxious about the unknown. I had heard many stories of India's epidemics, overwhelming crowds, and stifling pollution, and I had some fears about all the possible consequences. I decided to stop thinking about all the awful things that could happen and, instead, I sat still and listened to my inner voice. As I waited and listened, an overwhelming calm came over me, a calm that has always been a sign that I can trust my intuition. I knew that the unknown had powerful and surprising gifts for me, and that I wasn't alone. The same life source that guided me there in the first place was with me.

When the pilot announced that we would be landing in twenty minutes, I looked out the window and there she was: Mother India. There she was! I could not help but notice the dense, black air hovering above the land. I thought to myself, "Wow, I am going to be breathing all that into my lungs." At the same time, I had such excitement to actually land and touch my feet onto the soil of the land of my dreams.

To my surprise, India did not feel overwhelming or foreign at all. My visions had prepared me well. I went to the AID India office and joined the crew. Within a day, I was taken to Pondicherry on a long van ride filled with singing and laughing Buddhist monks. I felt a connection with a particular monk, Subogam, an orphan. He was a beautiful young man from Burma with a huge smile and some of the kindest eyes I had ever seen. Daniel, an old monk, had taken Subogam under his wing. They had come to southern India to help the tsunami survivors, too. At midnight, twelve of us were welcomed into an empty room with a marble floor and many mosquitoes. We used our sleeping bags as pillows, and the floor was the hardest bed I had ever slept on. I lay down near Daniel.

He said, "It's against the rules to sleep near a woman. But it's OK because we have a blanket of mosquitoes as our chaperones!"

We bonded because of our similar problem: Mosquitoes loved us. As a monk, he could not kill them, but he was relieved when I swung the mosquito zapper over him to kill off a few of the intruders.

We got our first look at the destruction in Thirukadaiyur. Before we arrived, we had already heard the unbelievable stories of the families who had lost their loved ones and their homes. When I walked through the villages, I was grateful to see that there was still a glimmer of light in many of the children's eyes.

As the day came to an end, I walked down a long road in the middle of the village. There were huts on each side. I began to skip down the road singing and, within minutes, a huge group of children was laughing and singing alongside me. We shared the common languages of laughter and song.

I decided that I would join Daniel and Subogam in a counseling group for the lowest caste village. We were sent to the most devastated village where the Dalits, or "broken people," live. Subogam was a big hit with the children. He was only seventeen years old, but had a depth that went beyond his years. He took off the top of his robe and began to play with the kids and teach them martial arts. The children screamed, "Jackie Chan! Jackie Chan!" I was fascinated that a village with no running water or television knew who Jackie Chan was. It was wonderful to see the joy in the kids' faces as they karate-chopped the air with Subogam.

A few minutes later, we were told that the body of an eight-year-old girl had just been found. Daniel, Subogam, and I began a long walk across a field of death. Many bodies had been retrieved there. I could smell the bleach powder used to kill off bacteria growing in the field. Once again, I felt that overwhelming sense of peace that I had come to rely on. This was to be the first time I would see a dead body, so I made each footstep a prayer as I got closer to the child.

I approached a man who was wearing a mask to fight the smell of decaying bodies. He told me he was studying to be a counselor and had volunteered for the relief efforts. He was in shock after having buried so many bodies day after day. He complained that the government refused to help in the recovery of the bodies because they were only Dalits. As we both looked down on the body of a little girl who had been half-eaten by dogs, I put my hand on his shoulder. I just wanted to reach out to him in the midst of his anguish, disappointment, and anger.

The little girl was so mangled that the only way the mother knew the child was hers was by the locket around her neck. As I began to walk away, I noticed the mother, crouched low to the ground. She began to scream and sob uncontrollably. Daniel and I knelt beside her. She buried her head into Daniel's saffron robe and I began to stroke her back. She cried in Tamil, "She was my only girl! She was my only girl!"

As my hand stroked her back, I could feel the vibrations of her grief resonating through her backbone. After a time, her sobbing ceased and we sat with her in silence. I looked into her eyes, not knowing what it is to be a mother, not knowing what it is to lose a daughter, but knowing what absolute agony looks and feels like. I realized then that loving deeply comes with the possibility of incredible pain and loss. I left the village that day vowing to love deeply, to live with an open heart, and to continue to live my dreams even when they led me to the brink of chaos and darkness.

When I got back to my motel, the yellowish, cold water I used for bucket showers looked like luxury, the simple food I ate was a feast, and the stained sheets I slept on were comforting; I had nothing to complain about.

The next day, I went back to be with Chandra, the mother of the little girl. She said, "If any of my children were to die, it was good that it was my daughter. I would not have been able to afford to marry her off. I am proud of my three boys because they all have jobs."

Later that day, I visited a fishermen's village. The villagers were in a higher caste than the Dalits. I was walking through their village when I came upon a huge pile of clothes that had been donated through tsunami relief efforts. I later found out that the clothes were burned because the villagers couldn't use them and just wanted to get rid of them. Kids were taking water packets that the relief effort gave them and squirting them on the ground and at each other. It was frustrating to see this when just ten miles down the road, people I cared about were not getting enough food and water. They could have used the clothes that were burned. The lowest caste received the least amount of help and attention from the government and would often go a day without clean water to drink.

On my last day, I bought more than one hundred cricket balls, crayons, and notebooks to take to the Dalit children. People from the United States had donated money for the gifts. I jumped in the back of a pickup truck and stood with twenty other volunteers.

The shock-less truck threw us back and forth over the dusty roads. As we bounced along, I felt a sense of gratitude—and the incredible feeling of being alive. When we arrived, we jumped off the truck and my fellow volunteers and I began to pass out the balls. The children and adults surrounded us, and I was suddenly in the midst of aggressive and excited people. It was intense to be surrounded by both children and adults begging for balls. None of the villagers were used to having material things other than necessities. What had felt like a good idea soon became overwhelming, but in the end, most of the children had received a cricket ball and were happily playing. A simple ball brought so much joy, and I spent the day playing catch with the children.

Our last day was a long one, and many of the relief workers were physically and mentally drained. We had bonded with each other, and parting would be bittersweet. A van came to take us out of the village. We asked the driver to meet us a few miles down the road. We all wanted to walk on the beach.

The sun was setting and we began to walk in the water. Within a few minutes we were all laughing and holding hands as we walked farther into the ocean, our clothes soaking wet. The same ocean that just weeks ago had engulfed whole towns and taken thousands of lives, the same water that had brought fear and destruction to the villagers, cleansed us and brought us joy.

Sacred Guidance

Della Clark

Wherever I am, God is!

—JAMES DILLET FREEMAN,
"Prayer for Protection"

With so many spiritual gifts blessing my life, I sometimes feel I am living several lives within this one. Some of the gifts arose during a passage through fear and pain. Others came as a shower of love and peace during a moment of divine Presence. I see both gifts as pieces of an initiation into the journey of remembering all that I am.

One January, while driving south on Highway 101 in California, I decided to visit a friend who wanted my instructions for building a sand labyrinth.

I knew he lived near Monterey, but I hadn't brought his address with me and his telephone number was not listed. Usually, I can find people easily, but this time, driving in circles, I was thwarted. I headed out of town. I had been on the rural mountain route to Interstate 5 many times in daylight and darkness, and knew it well. Though my intuition said to stay, I chose to go on.

It was almost sunset as I began the drive. After about an hour, in fog and a slight drizzle, I came upon yellow cones signaling roadwork. In the interest of safety, I decreased my speed. I saw no more cones as I traveled on, but suddenly, in the middle of a winding turn, I hit slick pavement. The road seemed to end, and the minivan became airborne. Everything slowed, and I remember thinking, "Oh, this is *that* time." I began James Dillet Freeman's "Prayer for Protection":

> *The Light of God surrounds me.*
> *The Love of God enfolds me.*
> *The Power of God protects me.*
> *The Presence of God watches over me. . .*
> *Wherever I am, God is!*

In blackness, I careened down the mountain through manzanita and over rocks. The van leveled out on a flat surface. Not knowing if another drop-off lay ahead, I braked just as the tires hit a large boulder. As the van rolled sideways, over and over again in slow motion, I could hear windows breaking. The noise was horrific as the side panels and the roof began to collapse, but my mind was calm. I understood that I must listen for guidance and not react. The car began to slide over a big sheet of rock and the roof was shifting. Then, everything stopped.

In the silence, I knew that I had chosen this particular reality, and I realized that the potential for injury was great. Those thoughts, however, did not arise from fear. It was an awareness that came from calm and presence.

I was hanging upside down by the seat belt in the seat that had been wrenched from its bolts. I was completely disoriented. I hung there for a long time and breathed deeply. I moved my hands and feet. I seemed to be OK. I was in a fetal position with the steering wheel at my knees, and I was tucked into what should have been the windshield, but was now a womb-like, dark space. The roof was folded over the windshield. Although it felt cold outside and it was raining, I was warm in the car.

I knew I could remove myself from the seat belt and lift the seat off my neck to relieve the discomfort, but I was acutely aware that I needed to listen for guidance. Then, I remembered that a spiritual message from many years ago had predicted this moment. The message had presented several different scenarios, one of which was better than the others. I tried to remember the outcomes. Which ended in severe injury or possible death? What did I need to do at this moment? In the silence, I heard, "Do not remove the seat belt!"

Feeling around in the darkness, I discovered that camping gear, dumped from the storage chest, was scattered across the ceiling of the car. I found a water bottle and began to hit the horn button with it whenever a car passed high above me on the road. I continued to honk the horn until the power died. Now, I was in total darkness.

I began to chant. Overtone chanting (chanting vowel sounds) clears my mind in preparation for meditation. I also use it to journey in a shamanic way to my guides and Teachers. I felt the vibrations of sound flowing through me. I visualized the Light flowing through me as I journeyed to my special place in non-ordinary reality. I asked my guides and Teachers to tell me how to get out of this situation in the way that would result in the highest good. "Listen and trust," they told me. "All is going to be well." I hugged my guides and Teachers, and returned from my journey, calm and present.

In the silence, I heard again, "Do not remove the seat belt!" Exploring in the darkness with my right hand, I found the charger cord for the cell phone. Was the cell phone in my purse or on the charger? I pulled the cord very slowly, because the connection was fragile, and there was a lot of debris on the car ceiling. Finally, the phone was in my hand. I could barely move my arm, but painfully, I dislocated my shoulder and forced its movement until my hand, with the phone, was on my stomach.

I dialed 911. I couldn't bring the phone to my

face, but when I heard the dispatcher's voice, I yelled, "HELP!" Mercifully, she heard me. She said someone could reach me in about an hour and, feeling instant relief, I hung up. Mistake! I called 911 again, and the dispatcher stayed on the line with me. I could taste blood, perhaps from hanging upside down for so long, and negative thoughts began to arise. Knowing that I couldn't hear guidance when my mind was filled with fear and confusion, I prayed that all my fearful and untrue thoughts would be transmuted into healing energy, and that this healing energy would be channeled to where it was most needed. As I prayed over and over, I began to feel peace.

Finally I saw the rescuers' lights—but they were going away from me. The dispatcher reassured me that the highway patrol officer could see my vehicle two hundred feet down the mountainside, but was zigzagging his way through the manzanita to reach me. When he did reach me, I think he was amazed to find me conscious and relatively uninjured.

The weather precluded a helicopter rescue, so a forestry rescue team fitted me with a neck brace and pulled me out through the windshield and onto the hood of a truck that was beside my van. The highway patrol officer had searched for me in the same area where that truck had also left the road. The driver had been on his way to a job, but he didn't return. He had survived the crash itself only to eventually die in the canyon. I believed that his spirit was still there. Through a healing meditation circle that I had facilitated for ten years, I had some experience assisting souls to the other side. I was able to send him on. I felt a tremendous release, as if a Karmic debt had been repaid.

It had been warm in the van, but it was cold outside in the rain. Although the rescue crew covered me with the blankets and a sleeping bag from my car, I felt frozen to the bone. I was grateful when they began winching me up the steep slope, with four of the forestry team guiding the litter.

Many people would blame the dangerous road for my accident, for being so poorly marked that two cars had left it in the same location. However, I believe I am responsible for *everything* that happens to me. Despite my own internal guidance to stay, I had chosen that road. I did not have to make that choice.

Cell phones do not work in the area where I went off the road. The highway patrol officer, the rescue team, the EMTs, the tow-truck driver, and the hospital staff all told me it was a miracle that I had found a signal. X-rays revealed that I had suffered only bruises and a dislocated shoulder. I was called "the Milagro," the Miracle Lady. I know that the experience occurred because it had a purpose.

After ten days of recuperating at home, I felt well enough to attend a workshop on Whidbey Island in Washington State. After I arrived, however, I felt confused, my attention was scattered and distracted, and I felt a profound drop in energy. I realized that part of my soul essence, in shock, was still at the site of the accident. I knew of the practice of soul retrieval, in which a shamanic practitioner journeys into non-ordinary reality for a person who has experienced trauma. They ride the vibrations of repetitive sound just as I do when I chant. They contact their helping spirits, animal totems, or guides to assist in locating the soul essence that departed the individual when they experienced the trauma. They may look in the realms of the earth—the lower world—or in the sky realms—the upper world—for these essence parts, which may appear as the person did at the age they experienced the trauma. Usually, when someone is curious enough to seek a soul retrieval, it is a signal that it is ready to return. Once found, the shamanic practitioner blows the essence into the heart and crown. This is a tradition that has been practiced for perhaps ten thousand years by diverse indigenous people across this planet. I arranged for one on my return home.

At the end of the workshop, I hitched a ride with another workshop attendee to the Seattle-Tacoma airport. As I was putting my suitcase in her rental car, I heard a snap and felt pain surge up my spine. Although it was more intense pain than I had ever experienced before, I continued on to the airport. As someone took my suitcase out of the rental car, I looked around and saw people coming from an employee door with a gate on the other side. I heard, "Go through the door." I do not know if this door actually exists, but I walked through it and then through the gate, feeling that spirit friends were guiding me. My flight was not scheduled to leave for several hours, but another one was leaving immediately, and I was able to get on it.

An examination revealed a compression frac-
ture at my third lumbar vertebra. The accident had ex-
acerbated my osteoporosis, leading to the injury that
had not shown previously on the X-rays. I remembered
the guidance I had received: "Do not remove the seat
belt!" If I had done so immediately after the accident,
that vertebra would have fractured while I was in the
canyon, and the outcome likely would not have been
good.

I know Great Spirit blessed me on many levels
with the gift of this experience. In the silent spaces of
no time, an opening occurred that connected me to
the strands of the future and the present, helping me
to prevent a devastating outcome. It confirmed to me
that this guidance is sacred.

I am grateful to my guides and Teachers in ordinary and non-ordinary reality, particularly those as-
sociated with the Foundation for Shamanic Studies. I
send blessings to all the angels in physical form, the
highway patrol and the forestry rescue team members
who risk their lives every day to assist those of us who
get into difficult situations. They are angels of God.

Hula, Seriously

Kristi Hager

'A'a i ka hula, waiho ka hilahila i ka hale.
Dare to hula, leave shyness at home.

—HAWAIIAN PROVERB

No, not Hula-hoops. Hula the dance. I have to clear this up immediately.

"We're going to dance a hula to the song 'Cool, Clear Water' at the Berkeley Pit."

I'm teaching as many people as I can to hula. I've been doing this dance for over a decade, alone in my painting studio overlooking the Pit in Butte, Montana, mostly to raise my spirits and keep warm in the dead of winter. Now, I want masses of us, dancing on the brink of this abandoned open-pit copper mine, a mile-

and-a-half across, rim to rim, that contains thirty-five billion gallons of contaminated water.

Most people intuitively know it's the right thing to do. It makes perfect sense to me. Hula is more than provocative pelvic movements packaged for sunscreen-slathered tourists at hotel luaus. Hula is ancient. Hula celebrates creation. Hula opens hearts. Hula goes to any level you want to take it. Hula heals.

But I don't say all of that stuff because I know that the whole notion of dancing hula beside a nine-hundred-foot-deep vat of poison is simply magnetic. I just say, "Next rehearsal, Tuesday night." And they come.

I am a circuit hula teacher now, traveling between Butte, Missoula, Helena, Bozeman, and Great Falls, gathering recruits for the Cool Water Hula. It would be nice if I could explain this to my mother.

"Mom, hula is my path, my Bliss, my Dharma Gate."

"Oh, is that what they are calling it these days?" she might say.

Even though I have considered the possibility that we might not be on paths, that we all might be just milling about, I'd rather surrender to my bliss than to my neuroses. Remember the feeling of giving in to helpless laughter? You are laughing so hard with a friend (it doesn't usually happen when you are alone) that you aren't laughing at the punch line anymore. It gets broader than that; you're laughing because you are laughing. And then you slip beyond laughter. It's funny

beyond your knowing *why* it's funny, and that keeps
you laughing, and pretty soon you aren't even laughing
at that. You are just *laughing*.

This is one definition of Bliss—being happy for
no reason. I used to laugh like this with my friends
when we got stoned, but I can't remember any of the
particulars. It's much groovier and more memorable
to have a laughing fit when you are straight and with
your mother. You enter a zone where the familiar social forms of mother and child drop away. You are just
two people sitting on the same couch, laughing. In the
zone, you abandon who you think you are for a while.
That is Bliss.

When I do hula, I can slip into that zone. I feel
open, willing to be seen, unguarded. I forget who I
think I am. I start smiling for no reason.

I want my mother to see me this way; really *see*
me, just once, with nothing hidden, with my sensual-
ity, my goofiness—all of it—out in the open. I decide
to do a hula for my mother's seventy-fifth birthday. My
sisters and their husbands, kids, and grandkids are all
gathered at the cottage on the Chesapeake Bay. The
sun is setting behind me, a perfect backdrop for hula.
This is my gift to Mom. My sisters are paying attention. Their spouses are being polite (this is cutting into
some pre-pre-season football game). Dad is napping.

But the grandkids are really digging it. They
are mesmerized. They start mimicking my moves. And
Mom. . . . I'm getting the same feeling I got when I gave
her my high school calligraphy project for Christmas,

a medieval illumination of the words, "Behold a Virgin shall conceive and bear a son and his name shall be called Emmanuel." Mom didn't really want to look at it very closely. And likewise, with my hula, she is taking it in peripherally. She seems just a little . . . who knows? Maybe she finds all this openness entirely too immodest. All I can say is that she seems happier when it's over and we get back to cake and ice cream. That moment I was looking for, when the roles of parent and child drop away—this is not one of those moments.

What words, what chain of events, what person put me on to hula? Probably not my mother, unless it was a logical rebellion against my Teutonic, Republican, Presbyterian, scientific method, and culturally un-diverse roots. Or other logical reasons such as healing my bad back, or that I am an Aquarian. This kind of reasoning is just a product of my mind, and therefore not deeply satisfying or reliable. To keep doing hula seriously, to involve friends and strangers in my brilliant scheme for healing the Pit, I need reassurance from beyond my own mind. I need revelation.

When I was nine years old, the community where our family lives decided to build a swimming pond, practically in our backyard, to be completed by the next summer. My mother was afraid of deep water. At close to forty years old, she had never learned how to swim. Now, with four kids, she was going to have to become our lifeguard.

She enrolled in a beginner's swim class at the Y from which I had graduated years ago. Starting that fall and every Saturday through the winter, she and I went to the Y. I was taking synchronized swimming. She was learning to breathe.

By spring, she progressed all the way through to senior life-saving. Since I am a strong swimmer, she practiced her technique on me. I would flounder in the deep end, pretending to drown. I got to throw a big thrashing fit, go into a blind panic, and legitimately try to strangle her. The wilder I was, the better. I was in heaven. Mom would wrestle and subdue me into a cross-chest carry or pull me by my hair, a legitimate lifesaving technique, to the edge of the pool, saved.

At the end of the class, she had to pass a written exam based on the *Red Cross Senior Life-Saving Manual*, a paperback with a green cover and a red cross in the center of a white circle and black block lettering below. I asked her the study questions listed at the end of each chapter. Mom answered by rote, having memorized the exact words of the text, reciting them back to me in a monotone. Here is where I am humbled and amazed at how the universe works: We never know when seeds are being planted or when they will spring forth, or when we ourselves are planting seeds in others. Whoever wrote the *Red Cross Senior Life-Saving Manual* had no idea their words would lead me to an ancient and holy celebration of life at the heart of America's biggest Superfund site.

One of the manual's memorable illustrations is of a swimmer with his head barely above water and snake-like weeds twining around both legs. In that time decades ago, I ask the manual's prescribed question, whose answer continues to live in me: "When swimming in a pond, what do you do if underwater weeds bind around your legs and pull you under?" My mother answers with the positive authority of catechism. "Extricate yourself with slow undulating motions." These words were not a part of my mother's normal waking vocabulary. And definitely not part of her body language, not that I had ever witnessed. These exotic words cast a spell. The second they were out of her mouth, we both burst into helpless laughter, the very first blissful laughing fit that I can remember having.

I am fifty years old. After a dark winter, I find myself at Easter time on a pilgrimage to the Merrie Monarch Hula Festival on the Big Island of Hawaii. I want to get to the source of a dance I've been doing alone for twelve years. I am surprised to find that Hilo is a working-class town, just like Butte. The festival is not on a manicured tropical lawn with waves breaking in the background; it is in a tennis stadium, a giant Quonset hut-shaped building, a half cylinder open on the ends. A raised platform the size of four boxing rings serves as the stage for the dancers with floor seating on three sides in folding chairs, then bleachers. From my spot on the bleachers, I can see Mauna Loa through the open end of the stadium. Though some thirty miles distant, the volcano presides over the festival, always visible behind the dancers.

After the grand procession, the blowing of a

conch shell, the National Anthem, the Hawaiian state song, and a prayer, the competition in ancient hula, *Hula kahiko*, begins. The first *halau*, school of hula, comes out on the platform to the beat of the calabash drum. This *halau* is all women. Their skirts are full. They wear modest, long-sleeved, full blouses. Their feet are bare. Wrists, ankles, and heads are adorned with halos of green leaves. The hula master begins chanting a tribute to the mountains, waterfalls, fish, flowers, gods, goddesses, Maui, and Pele. The dancers take up the chant in a call and response.

Thirty women move as one, gesturing to the sky and the ground, celebrating creation. Sometimes they are the ocean, sometimes they are flowing lava, mesmerizing everyone in the stadium. They leave the stage in a powerful surge. The man sitting next to me is weeping, too. "It's prayer," I say. He nods. These women allowed me, us, everyone to witness their souls speaking to God. We watch three more hours of public, embodied prayer. I don't know how the judges scored each hula. I rated them on how many hankies I needed. Three was tops.

By the third night of this, I am totally euphoric. Every cell of my body is full of hula. I go back to my motel room and fall into bed. I close my eyes. The whole bed is swaying, but the waves are inside me, as if I had spent all day in a small boat or swimming in the ocean, rocking in the waves. The waves of the dance come back. Words I haven't thought of in forty years come back to me like scripture: "Extricate yourself with slow undulating motions."

The festival is over. I don't know what to do with all this euphoria. In the morning, I check out of the motel and I find myself driving to Volcanoes National Park. I park the rental car in the main lot. As if pulled by a magnet, I walk to the front doors and right on through the Visitors Center, past the gift shop, the snack bar, the orientation video, directly out onto the observation deck. I'm looking straight into the caldera; it's a couple of miles across rim to rim, a magnificent circle of devastation going deep into the earth. I know this place, I know it in my bones. It looks just like the Pit. This place is sacred to the Hawaiians, and I see that however massively damaged, the Pit is sacred too. I know in my bones what I must do.

Four years later under a blue July sky, 156 of us line up for the Cool Water Hula on a flat-topped heap of crushed waste rock at the edge of the Berkeley Pit. A perfect breeze carries our 156 voices to at least as many onlookers gathered to witness this reverent, outrageous spectacle. As we begin our slow, undulating motions, the audience looks bemused at the unlikeliness: our numbers, our blue sarongs, our body language. After the first verse, "All day I face the barren waste without a taste of water, cool, clear water," I see subtle changes in their body language, a softening that signals a lump in the throat. By the last verse, "Way up there, please hear our prayer, teach us to care for water," the audience is beaming big-hearted smiles back at us—hula smiles. For a finale, we form a double conga line moving around the audience. When we come full circle, a cheer goes up, "Yahula!" A friend aims her video camera my way and all I can say is, "I am totally happy." It was a three-hankie hula. I am standing in a sea of euphoric people dressed in blue mingling with a sea of euphoric people not dressed in blue. We are humbled and amazed by the beauty of the moment after months of wondering what we would look like. We are very photogenic. We get great press.

Of course, the waters of the Pit were not instantaneously purified. It's hard for me to say exactly what happened. It feels so immodest. The slow, undulating motions are having a ripple effect I can't predict. I'm giving it up to God or Goddess, or whatever we're calling it these days. Many of us had an "in-body'" experience of communion. We felt relevant and connected. And we had fun, big fun. And isn't that the way it's supposed to be? Deep inside our sorrow and devastation, under all the up and down, good and bad, hard and soft, comes the smile for no reason.

Beyond the Riots

Diane Bock

People are unreasonable, illogical, and self-centered,
Love them anyway
If you do good, people will accuse you of
selfish, ulterior motives,
Do good anyway
If you are successful,
you win false friends and true enemies,
Succeed anyway
The good you do will be forgotten tomorrow,
Do good anyway
Honesty and frankness make you vulnerable,
Be honest and frank anyway
What you spent years building may be
destroyed overnight,
Build anyway
People really need help

but may attack you if you help them.
Help people anyway
Give the world the best you have
and you'll get kicked in the teeth,
Give the world the best you've got anyway

—"Anyway,"
from a sign on the wall of Shishu Bhavan,
MOTHER TERESA's children's home in Calcutta, India

In the wee hours one April morning, I staggered to my chair with my baby and flipped on the TV. The day before, I had been vaguely aware that the verdict was expected in the trial involving the Rodney King beating. What I witnessed on the TV during those events was horrifying. In hindsight, it transformed me.

I had always embraced the notion that all men are created equal. I knew the old sayings about not judging a book by its cover, that it's what's inside that counts. I knew that many people bore irrational grudges against others based on illogical stereotypes, but my imprecise impression was that racial prejudice was slowly diminishing. Although terrible things had happened in the past, I didn't think about race being a big issue today.

But the events leading up to the King trial made me realize, more forcefully than ever, that racism in any form is absurd. It's just plain dumb. I was horrified to understand that people—many people—are willing to *kill* because of skin color. They didn't know each other; they'd never even met. They had absolutely no reason to like or dislike one another.

My heart went out to a burly black man who sobbed as he watched his store burn to the ground. He kept repeating, "It's not right. It's just not right." And it wasn't right. He had been caught in the crossfire of ancient resentments, seething rage that lashed out and drew more innocents into the downward spiral of racism. He looked to be about fifty and was powerfully built, but he was as helpless as a small child, vulnerable and forlorn, with tears glistening on his cheeks. Swirling around him were smoke and flames, people running, screaming, and shouting, broken glass, gunshots blasting, sirens wailing. And there was nothing he could do to stop it. I imagined how powerless he felt.

From one hundred miles away, I knew that we are all vulnerable. The ugly forces of bitterness, ignorance, and fear can billow out to swallow up any number of innocent bystanders. Deliberate cruelty, ignorance, fear, and indifference . . . they all go into the recipe. And, like it or not, we all play a part.

How often we hear the phrase, "Somebody should do something about this!" But where do we find the "somebody"? Every once in a while, someone is motivated to do "something," rather than just talk about it. Unfortunately, most of these feelings tend to fade away as a busy life filled with distractions sets in.

But that wasn't the case for me this time. I stewed and brooded, haunted by the images of violence and hatred. I could not forget the storeowner. I still vividly remember what he was wearing, and how he had to stand by watching his livelihood and who knows how many years of work go up in smoke. And I wondered, "Is there something I can do?" How could I get people to spend enough time together to get to *know* each other? And if they could know each other, could I get them to *care* about each other? The whole picture changes and issues are very different when they affect someone that you care about personally. I wanted to take the fight against racism from the theoretical to the practical, to give people hands-on experiences with each other so they could form their own opinions and get beyond stereotypes. I prayed about several ideas and finally settled on a concept I called "Cousins."

Now, cousins are people that you don't necessarily see all that often. Usually, they are a little bit special; they are a constant. Through the years, you share pleasant experiences and special memories. My idea was to create connections among families of all races and provide enjoyable opportunities to interact in a natural family setting; to create easy, comfortable opportunities for people to forge genuine friendships across racial lines and, ultimately, to re-define "us" and "them."

Initially, I thought an existing organization would grab my idea and make it happen. After I wrote about a million letters offering the plan to various groups, my husband delicately pointed out to me that the likelihood of this coming true was very low. With great diplomacy, he challenged me, "If you want this to happen, you're going to have to do it yourself."

This took me aback. I had no idea how to actually *do* it. Talking about doing it was much easier. Nevertheless, I began. I applied to the IRS and got nonprofit status. I gathered advice and ideas. I recruited participants by distributing fliers and brochures at libraries, churches, schools, and pediatricians' offices. Sometimes, I would hand fliers to friendly-looking people at the grocery store. Most people were encouraging, but only a few actually signed up.

One day, a Latino church administrator told me she didn't want to know any white people because she didn't like them. I suggested I could match her with a black family; she still didn't sign up. I went home that day wondering, "What am I doing?"

I kept at it, though, and eventually collected enough willing pioneers to kick off the adventure. We held the first event in our backyard and got off to a terrific start with thirty-nine families. It was clear that many of the prospective participants were wondering whether this idea was for real. They were pretty sure there must be a catch. Many had very obviously been dragged there by their spouse. But they soon came to understand that the sole purpose of the program was to provide an easy opportunity for them to invest in each other with nothing specific required. On that first occasion, we had plenty of activities to draw people in and give them lots to talk about. There was a juggler, a painting table, a corny mixer game, a petting zoo, and terrific food. Our events are always potluck, and the Cousins tend to bring family favorites—homemade wontons, tamales, and trifle. Each family is matched with two sets of Cousins, so every Cousins family has a set of Cousins, and those Cousins have Cousins on the other side. This way, everyone is eventually connected in a chain reaction of Cousins.

We have forged fantastic friendships. We have a gathering once every couple of months, plus the Cousins are encouraged to get together on their own in any way that works for them. Some go to the movies, some play at the park or have a backyard barbeque. Many swap favorite recipes. Some pass along outgrown clothes and toys. These people were total strangers, and now they care about each other. They're sharing bits of themselves with each other and creating a common history for their kids. Each is working, in their own quiet way, to put a dent in the problem of prejudice. An extra-special moment occurred during our fifth anniversary celebration. We lined seventeen families up for a photo. As I glanced down the row, I got teary-eyed as I looked at the people who have grown so dear to me. The moms were busy chatting and the dads were joking around together. The kids were giggling and poking each other, actively engaged and obviously comfortable in each other's company. Many of these kids were toddlers when we started, and now they have grown up. They genuinely like each other.

You can tell by looking at them that they share special memories. They are birds of different feathers, flocking peacefully together. I looked around at the large extended hodge-podge of a family we created. This was the moment I realized we had really done it. We didn't just talk about it, we did it.

Many Cousins tell me that they're in it for life; they cannot imagine being without each other. They look forward to sharing the joys and sorrows to come, to attending the weddings of their Cousins' children and the funerals of their parents. And for some, it has been much, much more. One Cousin, a single, white mom, has done the legal work necessary so that if anything should happen to her, her daughter will be raised by her Cousins, a black, two-parent family of five. This is a unique case, but serves as a testimony to how important a Cousins connection can be. Who knows how far the ripples of goodwill created will travel?

I have frequently been asked, "Why are you doing this?" I feel this is what my heart called me to do. The haunting I felt when I saw the riots was a part of my soul's destiny to create change. This is something I'm capable of. I can make a difference in the world by being a friend and by promoting friendship. I don't have the resources to do a lot of things, but this is something within my capabilities. A favorite quote of mine by Edmund Burke is, "No one makes a bigger mistake than he who does nothing because he could only do a little." Barriers have gone up between people brick by brick, and I believe that's the way they are most likely to come down: one person at a time. If I can help a few barriers come down, perhaps that is the small role I was meant to play in the endless possibilities for connection. I know we're smart enough to figure out how to be good to each other.

Recently, I faced a scheduling conflict when an old family friend died and his memorial service was scheduled for the same time that I was co-hosting a baby shower for one of our Cousins. Not wanting to miss either, we decided that my husband and daughters would assume my hostess duties at the beginning of the shower while I attended the service, and then I would rush back to join them as quickly as possible.

As I made the twenty-minute drive from the service to the shower, I cried for a number of reasons. I mourned the loss of a dear friend and grieved for his family. They were neighbors of my family and I had known them all my life. I have a permanent connection with them, forged early in my life and nurtured through years by positive interactions and shared events—neighborhood get-togethers, birthday parties, graduations, weddings, baby showers. They were always there. And now one of them would not be.

Dozens of familiar faces from my neighborhood had greeted me at the service, many of them considerably older than the last time I had seen them. And it occurred to me that I would likely be attending more funeral services in the next few years. This made me sad, too.

Although I didn't think much about it at the

time, I realize now how lucky I was to grow up in a caring community where neighbors invest in each other, take an interest in each other's kids and remain a part of each other's lives decade after decade. I contemplated how rare that is now, and lamented that my kids are not growing up in such an idyllic setting. The world is different and my old neighborhood is different, too. Even if we moved back there, we wouldn't be able to re-create the same sort of environment. This also made me sad. And I wished that my kids could have a set of grown-up friends like the ones I'd had, that would be a constant source of stability and encouragement for them.

As I made the final few turns, hastening to get to the baby shower, I realized that, in fact, my kids *do* have a version of what I had, and I was rushing to that setting at this very moment. Our Cousins represent a set of families remarkably similar to the neighbors I grew up with. We don't all live on the same street and we don't look as homogeneous, but we have the same sort of companionable interactions. We are investing in each other for the long haul, and the fact that we have such varied backgrounds makes the mix all the more rich. My sorrow eased and was partially replaced with gratitude for being so fortunate when I was a child— and continuing to have such good fortune now that I am a parent.

My husband and I thought that we were doing this for mankind. We didn't think we needed Community Cousins. We gave them an open door—

and they blessed us with joy that comes from belonging to this unique and colorful family. My own family has come to realize that, in fact, we are the luckiest of all.

Prayer in Action

Jyoti

In this time of movement, where celestial doors have opened, we must do what we have been asked to do. We are standing in the movement and the vibration of a sacred prophecy. The prophecy tells us that consciousness is preparing the spirit of the feminine, the spirit of the Grandmothers. It is in the prophecy that we shall walk into the light united from the four directions.

—FLORDEMAYO,
Mayan Grandmother, Highlands of Central America

We land in New Delhi, India, and take a van to Dharamsala, the second home of the Tibetan people. The drive takes two days over curving, narrow roads that wind up into the mountains. Grandmother Tsering, an elder of the Tibetan people, and her son Gelek are traveling with my two friends and me. We have come to prepare for the arrival of The International Council of Thirteen Indigenous Grandmothers. But first, let me take a moment to reflect on what has brought us here.

On October 11, 2004, thirteen indigenous grandmothers from all over the world—Alaska; North, South, and Central America; Africa; and Asia—arrived at the Tibet House mountain retreat in upstate New York for the Global Women's Gathering. They were responding to prophecies handed down through generations of their own people that spoke of a time when they would be called together for the sake of Mother Earth and all of her children.

This first council gathering was a time of hope and inspiration. The Grandmothers are women of prayer and women of action. Their traditional ways link them with the forces of the Earth. Their solidarity with one another creates a web that serves to balance the impact of injustices wrought by an imbalanced world—a world disconnected from the fundamental laws of nature and the original teachings based on a respect for all life.

Starting at that first gathering in New York, the Grandmothers successfully formed an international alliance unlike any the world has ever seen. The thirteen elders agreed to sit in council, each representing her own traditions, ceremonies, lineages, countries, and languages. As a result of these actions, they formed a visible bond that many believe will inspire others to pray and act for unity and peace on Earth.

The Global Women's Gathering was created as a way to bring women elders together to form the Grandmothers Council. In 2002, I was introduced to Bernadette Rebienot, a Bwiti elder and Grandmother of the people in Gabon. I had traveled to Gabon to speak with her about a way of healing. I came to learn that Grandmother Bernadette, advisor to the president of Gabon and a spiritual elder respected by many for her healing work, shared a common vision held by me and the community—to establish an international council of indigenous spiritual women leaders. During our first meeting, I shared with her a vision that had been brought to my own spiritual community in 1998. Our Divine Mother appeared and said, "I am going to give to you one of my most precious baskets. Inside it, I am going to place my most precious jewels. They represent lines of prayer and ways of life that reach back to the original times. Do not change them. Do not mix them. Preserve them and keep them safe and walk them through the doorway of the millennia. I have something we are going to do."

The whisperings of this vision began to speak of a prophecy that tells about a time when North America and South America were one body of land. Then, there were great changes on the Earth and the land split. The prophecies say there would come a time when the Peoples of these two lands would share their holy smoke together—a time when the eagle and the condor would once again fly together. When this happens, the new world of unity is opening itself to us. And that is what occurred. The medicine peoples of these lands began to share what their way of life was teaching them. The forest was their teacher. The plants were their teachers. All of creation was directly involved in a way of life that taught sustainability and unity. Each person carried a similar story through their prophecy and through their songs that spoke of the times that challenge us, and what we must do to walk through them and into the new world. It took two years after our meetings with Grandmother Bernadette and two other Grandmothers from the Amazon Rainforest in Brazil, Maria Alice and Claire, before my community and I would meet in New York with the Council of Grandmothers. We knew these elder women would have the knowledge to guide us in returning to a way of life that would preserve these old traditions, and a way of life that would sustain our Earth and life on Her.

While we were meeting in New York, Grandmother Rita Pitka Blumenstein from the Yup'ik tradition in Alaska, who is in her seventies, told us a story that confirmed our vision. She said that when she was nine years old, her grandmother said to her, "When you are old like me, you will be called to sit on a council of thirteen grandmothers. I have made you thirteen sacred bundles. Inside each, I have placed one of my most precious stones. I have gathered thirteen eagle feathers. When the time comes, you are to pass

out these bundles and eagle feathers to each grandmother and sit down and take one for yourself. Know
that I am standing behind you. The new time coming,
as foretold by our ancestors, has arrived. Know that we
are standing behind you."

All felt a time of destiny was at hand because
these precious prayer bundles are gifts that hold
great spiritual meaning to their tribes. They had each
been prepared in a traditional and sacred way for the
Grandmothers. They would empower their actions.
The bundles were clear manifestations to us of the
Mystery and its sacred ways guiding us.

The gathering in New York provided a rare
opportunity for women of different races, ages, backgrounds, and professions to hear the experiences, stories, and unique insights of others representing their
indigenous ancestry. It also offered three hundred
participants a unique opportunity to witness a panel
discussion in which the indigenous elders and leading
women from Western cultures—Carol Moseley Braun,
Helena Norberg-Hodge, Tenzin Palmo, Gloria Steinem,
Luisah Teish, and Alice Walker—examined the global
challenges confronting us and explored what can be
done to help sustain the planet by cultivating a balanced way of life.

Together the women addressed the major challenges now facing us: How do we ensure the health
and well-being of ourselves and our families? How do
we heal and protect our precious planet? How do we
maintain our connection with Spirit in the face of this

political environment? How do we help to bring peace and accord to the communities in which we belong?

As Grandmother Clara Shinobu Iura from the Amazon Rainforest in Brazil said, "In these latest times we live in, when killing seems almost natural, we are here in these days of prayer so that we can illuminate a consciousness for this planet that is in agony. Inside our hearts, I believe each of us present at this gathering feels great hope. This is a seed being planted."

The gathering sought to heighten our awareness of indigenous traditional cultures and their healing ways. It helped us see how we can extend and sustain these invaluable traditions into the foreseeable future. As the women elders shared their traditional stories, we began to envision how we could make these values operative in our contemporary cultures.

The Grandmothers came to the table with open hearts. They took the time to learn deeper levels of respect for one another by listening and speaking through the cultural and linguistic barriers. They came with no agenda about what would happen next. They faced each other in a circle as they formed the first International Council of the Thirteen Indigenous Grandmothers. When you add up their collective ages, they represent almost nine hundred years of feminine wisdom. As individuals, each possesses wisdom about life, gained through time, spiritual gift, and practice, which guides their peoples. Together as a council, their wisdom is multiplied into a voice that can be heard above the chaos prevalent in the world at this time.

They decided to hold a prayer for world peace by hosting gatherings every six months, traveling to one another's home places to cultivate their unified voice. In spring 2005, the Grandmothers Council met at the home of the Mayan Grandmother Flordemayo in Pojoaque Pueblo, New Mexico. In May 2006, the Grandmothers visited Mazatec Grandmother Julieta Casimiro in Oaxaca, Mexico. And in October 2006, they met in Dharamsala, India, and held a private audience with His Holiness the Dalai Lama. It was during this audience that His Holiness recognized the work in the world that the council was doing as it called prayer into action. Our alliance was strengthened when the minister of culture for the Tibetan people said, "His Holiness would find it a great privilege to be considered one of the jewels in Her basket."

We went into Dharamsala with our prayer held as a sacred intent. Grandmother Tsering wanted us to focus on softening the hearts of the Chinese people so that His Holiness could return to his country before his death. She felt that if he did not return home, then her people would never be able to return. We were amazed at the courage and spiritual strength of the Tibetan people. The Dalai Lama says that the Chinese people have come to teach them about compassion—that the subjugation of their homeland is an opportunity to embody the teachings of compassion while sustaining their culture and their way of life. And that is what we found.

The night the Grandmothers' buses arrived,

lightning streaked across the sky. Because one of the buses had had a flat tire, they all arrived four hours late. Yet several hundred people—children, nuns, officials—all waited with an excitement that filled the air. "The Grandmothers are coming!" The night before their arrival, a nun and her two children had been shot trying to escape from Tibet into Dharamsala. And the last night they were there, two more people were shot trying to escape to freedom.

As the Grandmothers lit their sacred fire and held their seven-day prayer vigil for world peace and unity, the challenges to peace confronted us continually. There were so many ways we could have misunderstood one another. There were seven languages being translated simultaneously. There were thirteen individuals, each walking with her own history and wounds. There were thirteen different lines of prayer, one to represent each of the Grandmothers' cultures. And still, they came to sit with and learn from one another.

Over the last few years as the prayer has continued to unfold, there have been many tests. Our material world has grown out of the genocide of first-nation peoples around the world. That material world has based itself on a model of scarcity and fear. It has defined itself through the conquest of land and the people on it. It has disassociated itself from the Earth as a living, breathing being and intellectualized its relationship with Nature. Our political positions have been a direct result of this disconnection, producing belief systems that are myopic in nature and separate us, rather than uniting us as a global village. We have forgotten how to talk with Creation; we have lost our way.

But we have reached a moment of humility that if we have the courage to embrace it, we will dream a new dream for our children and grandchildren. If we cannot step out of our egos and into the heart of our Spirit, then we will continue to invest in ways that are threatening the very health of the planet and her inhabitants.

While I was praying in Dharamsala, I was shown a vision: I saw the great tree of life growing up through this reality. Life abounded in it and under it. All life was nourished from it. All life was sheltered by it. Then, a great time of challenge came. Something cut the tree down near its roots.

The first-nation peoples are this tree's roots. The genocide was the knife that cut. The top of the tree was almost severed from its roots. It had almost been completely severed from its source, except for one small strand. As the Grandmothers make their way around the table for peace and unity, they bring healing to the tree through their prayers, unified in a respect for all life and all peoples. As each Grandmother hosts these gatherings in her home place, those prayers have gone before and awaken in her people a memory of the time when the tree was whole. At that moment, the illness of our time, or whatever needs to be healed, rises up and threatens the health of the council in such a way that they must put peace into practice. As some of our Grandmothers say, carrying a prayer for peace is very difficult in this day and time because that which does not want peace will confront it. But we are not here to fight for peace; we are here to *be* peace. We must embrace that which challenges us and pray for those who are not at peace. If we can hold peace without needing to explain it, if we can forgive the history and the story of that which brought it, and if we can keep our focus on the prayer for unity, then another place on the wounded tree of life can heal. If we can stay rooted in our commitment to peace, then the prayer will continue to move on.

I was shown that tree, standing healed and whole, supporting life again, with our renewed relations in dialogue with the Original Grandmother—the one who has no relations, the one who dreamed it all.

Many of the Grandmothers travel to these gatherings at great risk to their own health. I remember when Grandmother Aama had to walk through bombs going off just to get to the airport. She wasn't even sure she would be allowed to travel by air because her country was in such upheaval when members of the royal family in Nepal were overturned. But she felt she was protected as her plane took off to bring her to the gathering in Mexico. Several of the Grandmothers have had health problems and other issues that could have kept them home, but their dedication to world prayer was stronger.

What I discovered along the way is that we are

not women of politics, we are women of prayer. We are grandmothers who are taking what Grandmother Agnes, from the Takelma-Siletz tribe in Oregon, says is the most important journey of our time: "that fourteen inches from our heads to our hearts."

The old ones say that there is a story stalking each of us and, when we are ready, it pounces on us to speak through us. For me, this walk began when I was a young girl of the South. I could not understand why some people were treated differently because of the color of their skin or where they lived. Martin Luther King said, "I have a dream!" And it is that dream that changed our reality. I heard a small voice whisper, "When the Grandmothers speak!" And that has changed my reality.

When I listen to the news or hear the stories of the many wars and inhumanities occurring today, I can get overwhelmed and feel hopeless. But if I listen to Creation and follow the vision She has shown us, then I am able to act out of the love I have for this Earth and the love I hold for my grandchildren. It brings me back to our Original People who are the guardians of this planet. They have a way of life that sustains life.

If we can return to that way of life, we will find a way back to ourselves. When something unsettles us, we will look inside to see where it resides in us. We will begin to remember the world is as we dream it.

When this all began, I had no idea that it would grow into what some are calling a global movement. I was a woman born in the South. At times, there was talk about a Cherokee grandmother, but this was something not to be talked about. I didn't understand my history or the history of our country and what had happened to the Original People of this land. I was a woman who was born at the end of World War II with a wave of "baby boomers." As we grew, we began to question the box; we began to test the box; we began to redefine the box. We awoke in the middle of dysfunction and, instead of denying it, we embraced it and began to heal it—first, on a personal level, then on a generational level, and now on a global level. Grandmothers all over the planet are beginning to stand up. We are their prayer in action.

As Grandmother Rita Blumenstein says, "The past is not a burden; it is a scaffold which brought us to this day. We are free to be who we are—to create our own life out of our past and out of the present. We are our ancestors. When we can heal ourselves, we also heal our ancestors, our grandmothers, our grand-fathers, and our children. When we heal ourselves, we heal Mother Earth."

About the Contributing Authors

LAUREN ARTRESS is author of *Walking a Sacred Path: Rediscovering the Labyrinth as a Spiritual Practice*, *The Labyrinth Seed Kit*, and *The Sacred Path Companion: A Guide to Walking the Labyrinth to Heal and Transform*. She is founder and creative director of Veriditas: The World-Wide Labyrinth Project, a 501(c)(3) committed to facilitating the transformation of the human spirit. Lauren is a licensed MFT psychotherapist in California, an Episcopal priest, and honorary canon of Grace Cathedral. She is an effective motivational speaker.

Web sites:
www.laurenartress.com • www.veriditas.org

CHRISTINA BALDWIN is a writer, seminar presenter, keynote speaker, and spiritual activist. She believes that everybody has a story, and that story is the voice of humanity. Reclaiming the place of story is the core of her life work, for she believes we weave the world from

the story outward. She has written many books about the importance of tracking our life stories, the empowerment of journal writing, and creating ways to speak and listen to each other with heartfelt respect. She and PeerSpirit co-founder Ann Linnea travel extensively to lecture, teach, and call people and organizations into conversations of heart and meaning. In the past few years, they have journeyed across the U.S. and Canada, England, Denmark, Greece, Germany, Zimbabwe, and South Africa to create spaces where people's truest stories can be heard. Christina currently lives on an island near Seattle, Washington. Her most recent book is *Storycatcher: Making Sense of Our Lives through the Power and Practice of Story*. She and Ann also wrote a book together, *The Circle Way: A Leader in Every Chair.*
Web sites:
www.peerspirit.com • www.storycatcher.net

DIANE BOCK was raised in Los Angeles, twelve miles from the neighborhood where the riots broke out. She graduated from University of Southern California with a degree in business and then lived for two years in London, working for Carnation Co., after which she returned to Los Angeles, working at jobs in advertising and publishing. In 1986, she married Larry Bock and they moved to the San Diego area three years later. The Bocks have two daughters. Diane retired in 1992 in order to devote herself to family, but has been spending a good deal of time founding and running Community

Cousins. Cousins play a special part in the lives of her children and she's happy to have added many, many Community Cousins to their sphere.

In 1999, Community Cousins was selected by Vice President Al Gore as one of ten outstanding grassroots efforts nationwide. Oprah published a story about the group in her magazine in July 2000. NBC produced a lengthy news feature about the program that went on to win a Peabody Award.

Web site: www.cuzz.org

KRISTI MEISENBACH BOYLAN is the author of *The Seven Sacred Rites of Menopause: The Spiritual Journey to the Wise Woman Years*, *The Seven Sacred Rites of Menarche: The Spiritual Journey of the Adolescent Girl*, and *Born to Be Wild: Freeing the Spirit of the Hyperactive Child*. She lives in Parker, Texas.

E-mail: boylanvoice@yahoo.com

Born in Chile in 1944, **JOSEFINA BURGOS** fled the Chilean dictatorship of General Pinochet in 1976 and came to the United States with her son and husband. She lived in Washington, D.C., where she worked as an architect for sixteen years and was able to forget the nightmare in Chile, although the "presence" she had felt never quite left her. When she moved to San Francisco in 1992, she found herself embarked on "a long and painful search for my lost soul," which led her to the California Institute of Integral Studies. Through the experience of her studies in archetypal psychology, philosophy, and religion, she was able to open the long-closed door to her soul and move forward on the path that led her toward wholeness and a reconnection with her dreams. Now she is actively writing and lecturing on the subject of meaning and imagination. She has obtained a master of arts degree in philosophy and religion, and is currently completing studies toward her doctorate.

E-mail: jburgos@igc.org

MARCELLINE BURNS, PhD, spent thirty years as a research psychologist. She retired at the end of 2003 and now explores the vast possibilities of leisure time. She lives at the beach, and finds daily spiritual sustenance with family and friends, books, and walks beside the sea. She travels to remote locations, and feels blessed to experience the wonder of this earth and its animals and peoples. With ever so slight a sense of regret, she acknowledges that there are more magical places to visit than time will allow.

E-mail: mburns4430@roadrunner.com

DELLA CLARK is a marriage and family therapist and a spirit-walker in Mount Shasta, California. With the assistance of her guides and Teachers, she teaches journeying skills and chanting workshops, and does soul retrievals and death and dying work. She works outside of time with her students and clients to assist in the manifestation of their healing, and offers support to those who have had psychic awakenings or spiritual visitation. Della enjoys taking individuals and small groups on sacred healing walks of special places on Mount Shasta.

Web site: www.spiritwalkersretreat.com
E-mail: hidella@aol.com

ALICE BUTLER COLLINS is a writer, storyteller, workshop facilitator, educator, and mother. She spent thirty-seven years working as an educator in Chicago public schools. She held positions as a teacher, supervisor, administrator, principal, due process coordinator, and as liaison to the Office for Civil Rights. She enjoys travel, reading, theater, and sports. Writing enables her to share her passion for the power of the written and oral word with a diverse audience.

Web site: www.alicebutlercollins.com
E-mail: arbcoll@sbcglobal.net

BOBBI GIBB is a lawyer, artist, writer, philosopher, and mother. The inspiration for all she has done comes from her spiritual sense of life, the beauty and mystery of nature, and the wonder of the human experience. Bobbi became the first woman to run the Boston Marathon in 1966. She ran again in 1967 and 1968 and placed first in the women's division. She was inducted into the Road Runners Club of America Hall of Fame in 1982.

Web site: www.bobbigibb.com

KRISTI HAGER lives in Missoula, Montana, and has worked as a self-employed photographer and multi-disciplinary artist since 1984. She was a presenter at the Art, Culture, Nature Conference in Flagstaff, Arizona, in 2001. In 2003, Hager received a Gottlieb Foundation Individual Support grant based on her twenty years of artistic achievement. StoryCorps featured her audio tribute to her mother on National Public Radio in February 2006. Her book, *Evelyn Cameron: Montana's Frontier Photographer,* was selected by the Montana Book Awards as an honor winner in 2007.

In the early 1980s, Hager lived in the Bay Area and took hula lessons on a whim. The dance changed her art and her life. In 2000, she produced, directed, and choreographed a live performance titled "Cool Water Hula: An Art Action," and produced a video documenting this event. The story of the Cool Water Hula is now a part of a history book for all middle school students in Montana.

Web sites:
www.cultivatedbabes.com • www.kristihager.com
E-mail: kristi@montana.com

COLLEEN HAGGERTY lost her leg in an auto accident when she was seventeen years old. The journey of her disability has taught her about the power of her spirit and how it guides her body through this lifetime. She is a trained SoulCollage™ facilitator, a process that guides people to their inner wisdom. As a trained life coach, Colleen coaches and mentors at her job at Big Brothers Big Sisters of Northwest Washington. She lives in Bellingham with her husband, two children, and her goofy dog.

E-mail: haggertyrobinson@msn.com

S. KELLEY HARRELL, CHt, is an author, columnist, and neoshaman living in North Carolina. Her book, *Gift of the Dreamtime: Awakening to the Divinity of Trauma*, chronicles her pivotal steps into her role as a shaman. She writes the syndicated column "Intentional Insights," and has written for *SageWoman*, *If . . . Journal*, and the *Beltane Papers*, and is published in several anthologies. She is an Ascension Reiki and Usui Reiki Ryoho Master and Teacher walking the path of the modern Druid.

As the co-president of the Saferoom Project, a non-profit support network for sexual assault survivors and their partners, family, and friends, Kelley helped to found the group in 1998. She makes her home with a wonderful lover and their two energetic children. A passionate animist, her shamanic practice is Soul Intent Arts, and she is vigorously involved with the world in and around her.

Web sites:
www.intentionalinsights.com • www.kelleyharrell.com
www.soulintentarts.com

MAMA DONNA HENES, as she is affectionately called, is an internationally renowned urban shaman, award-winning author, popular speaker, and workshop leader whose joyful celebrations of celestial events have introduced ancient traditional rituals and contemporary ceremonies to millions of people in more than a hundred cities since 1972. She has published four books, a CD, an acclaimed quarterly journal, and writes online for the Huffington Post and UPI's Religion and Spirituality forum. Mama Donna maintains a ceremonial center, spirit shop, ritual practice, and consultancy in Exotic Brooklyn, New York, where she works with individuals, groups, institutions, municipalities, and corporations to create meaningful ceremonies for every imaginable occasion.

Web sites:
www.donnahenes.net • www.thequeenofmyself.com

JYOTI (Jeneane Prevatt, PhD) is one of the founders of Kayumari, a spiritual healing community located in the Sierra foothills of California, the redwoods of the Black Mountain Preserve Retreat Center between Jenner and

Cazadero, California, and in New York, Switzerland, Prague, and the Amazon. She is the spiritual director of the Center for Sacred Studies, a church dedicated to protecting and sustaining the spiritual practices of first-nation peoples around the world as they join their hearts in a prayer for world peace. From that effort, the International Council of Thirteen Indigenous Grandmothers has evolved. Jyoti is an internationally renowned spiritual adviser and psychological consultant. Her background includes education in cross-cultural spiritual practices, social services program development, training at the Jung Institute in Switzerland, and extensive international travel. She has devoted her life to bringing unity to the planet by facilitating the development of alliances between individuals who are the guardians of indigenous culture and traditional medicine ways.

Web sites:
www.cssministryofprayer.org
www.forthenext7generations.com
www.grandmotherscouncil.com
www.mothersgrace.com • www.sacredstudies.org

GLADYS McGAREY, MD, MD(H), has been a family physician for over sixty years. She is internationally known for her pioneering work in holistic medicine, natural birthing, and the physician-patient partnership. A founding member and past president of the American Holistic Medical Association, she also serves on a research committee of the National Institute of Health's Office of Alternative Medicine. She is a member of the International Advisory Board for the recently formed Institute for Natural Healing. Her work, through the Gladys T. McGarey Medical Foundation, has helped to expand the knowledge and application of holistic principles through scientific research and education. She lectures internationally and is the author of many articles and books.

Web sites:
www.isupportholistic.com
www.mcgareyfoundation.org

ALISON NORMAN completed her master's degree in counseling education at the University of San Diego. She has been cancer-free since 1997 and is working as a high school counselor. She believes that her struggle has made her an empathetic counselor who is comfortable and passionate when working with individuals who have challenges.

E-mail: alisonnormanma@gmail.com

Singer, songwriter, poet, educator, writer, and presenter, **SUNI PAZ** has devoted her life to children and their families. She has thrilled worldwide audiences of all ages on stage, television, and radio with her stories in song accompanied on guitar, charango, and percussive instruments. Born in Argentina, she lived in Chile for five years and then moved to the United States with her children. She received a master's degree at Rutgers University in Hispano-American literature; a grant from the Center for International Education; and Fulbright, Atlas, Tinker Foundation, and several other awards. The latest was the Parents' Choice Award for a children's CD with the Smithsonian Institution.

Since 1984, she has been involved in an ongoing collaboration with award-winning writers and poets Alma Flor Ada and Isabel Campoy, setting their lyrics to music and recording them. She has recorded and published more than four hundred songs. In 2007, Del Sol Books published her memoirs in Spanish, *Destellos y sombras*, and in English, *Sparkles and Shadows*. Five of her poems are in a book entitled *La sublime locura de ser poeta*. Suni believes in the art and power of music and words to change, inspire, and heal.

Web site: www.sunipaz.com

HAGIT RA'ANAN is deeply dedicated to working for peace. She uses her background in education, public relations, and healing to work with children and adults with the hope of breaking the cycles of hatred, fear, and mistrust. She lives to create bridges of peace between societies in the Middle East, and between people of different faiths.

Web sites:
www.bridgesofpeace.org
www.jerusalempeacemakers.org

JANET GRACE RIEHL is an award-winning author, artist, and performer. Her first book, *Sightlines: A Poet's Diary*, is also available as an audiobook, *Sightlines: A Family Love Story in Poetry and Music*. Janet's poems, stories, and essays have been published in national literary magazines and anthologies. She is a member of the Authors Guild and is registered with Poets and Writers. From St. Louis, Janet frequently crosses the Mississippi to partner with her ninety-four-year-old father on musical and literary projects. Her blog-magazine, Riehl Life: Village Wisdom for the 21st Century, is dedicated to creating connections through the arts and across cultures.

Web site: www.riehlife.com
E-mail: janet.riehl@gmail.com

SHERI RITCHLIN is a writer, lecturer, and dream worker who does much of her writing and dreaming in her camper, Mr. Fields, currently perched in Sonoma County, California. She came to the Bay Area from Del Mar, California, to enter the California Institute of Integral Studies, where she completed her dissertation—*The Return of the Sage: A New Cosmology Meets the Way of Heaven and Earth in the I Ching*—under the guidance of Yi Wu, Richard Tarnas, and Brian Swimme. She is the author of *One-ing* and *Dream to Waken*, as well as articles published in *Parabola, Noetic Sciences Review, A Tribute to Thomas Berry*, and *The Evolutionary Epic: Science's Story and Humanity's Response*. She is currently at work on *Fields of Light: 2012 and the Venus Transit of the Sun.*

Web site: www.sheriritchlin.com

EVE STRELLA is CEO of Strella & Associates, a company focused on coaching, consulting, keynoting, training, team energizing, and industrial engineering. She holds a bachelor's degree in industrial engineering. Eve is a published author of numerous articles and contributor to several books. She routinely writes for *Leadership Excellence* and *Personal Excellence* on topics of business, fear in the workplace, positive thinking, and much more. She is a keynote speaker, and lectures on many cruise lines where she educates and entertains the passengers. Equestrian sport (dressage), astronomy, photography, writing, painting, jewelry-making and pottery are her passions. Eve and her husband Ed love to spend starry nights in their backyard observatory exploring the universe and doing astrophotography.

Web sites:
www.evestrella.etsy.com
www.linkedin.com/pub/2/978/294
www.stardustobservatory.com
www.strellaandassociates.com
E-mail: estrella@estrellaandassociates.com

NICOLETTE TAL grew up in Milwaukee, Wisconsin, and Santa Barbara, California. She received her undergraduate degree from Pomona College and her law degree from Santa Clara University, where she met her husband, Ron Ball. They lived and practiced law in the San Francisco Bay area, where their two children were born. In 1986, they moved to San Diego County.

Nicolette obtained her scuba diving license as a prerequisite for her marriage license and enjoyed being Ron's dive buddy until their children were big enough to take her place. She gave up her law practice in 1997, when she was diagnosed with a motor neuron disease. She lived at home in Solana Beach, where she remained involved with her family, book club, and other friends, and did a little writing until her death on August 30, 2004.

JENNIFER THOMPSON TREPANIER has a master's degree in psychophysiology, and a passion for helping people unlock their potential. She gives inspirational talks and counsels the chronically ill. Jennifer is deeply interested in the stories of others and believes that traveling the world is a gift for her spirit. She is currently writing a book that focuses on women and the power and wisdom behind their so-called physical "flaws." One of her passions is volunteering with hospice organizations. She appreciates the wisdom she receives from tending to the dying.

Web site: www.wellsofwisdom.com
E-mail: jen@wellsofwisdom.com

Acknowledgments

I send deep gratitude to my tribe, my inner circle of treasured people, who enabled me to deliver the healing stories that you hold in your hands. The most important men in my life encircled me: my husband Lee Gopadze and my son Paul. I also thank Peter László (the computer guru). They were faithful contributors, even when they thought I had gone a bit mad in my search for stories that reflected the wisdom of the divine feminine. They gave me the strength and courage to carry on during the many years it took to complete this book.

My heartfelt gratitude goes to Marcelline Burns and Sheri Ritchlin, who nurtured this book from inception until it became a reality. Your devotion is forever cherished and can never be repaid. I am very grateful for the intuition of Angeles Arrien, who could "see" that this book was "guided," and wrote the wise and inspiring foreword.

I give thanks to my late mother, Edna Stark, who watches over me, and who taught me to love stories. My respect goes to my late father, whose kindness and teachings to be open to people of all beliefs greatly influenced my life.

I am grateful for the collective wisdom of my dear friends including Paul Bombolian, the book's father spirit; Carolyn and Lester Stein, who helped me every step of the way; Sue Lavin; Wendy Giss; Jonelle, who *gave* me the idea; and Gordon Reynolds, Anne Mery, Tammera Logan, Tamara Brandon, Kenneth Miller, Shirley Gram, Ali Norman, Tiffany Norman, Debbie Johnson, Karen Taylor, Audrey Oh, Eleanor Connelly, Moonflower, Cay Randall-May, Shirley McKinley and Doris Leit, who all gave of their time and gifts and went above and beyond the call of friendship!

My appreciation goes to each author for evoking loving kindness, authenticity, truth, forgiveness, and courage. Your lives show that you are active conduits between the human and the invisible world. Through your stories, we can all travel the many paths of spirit into beautiful moments of transformation.

Contributing editors Marcelline Burns, Susan Clotfelter, Sheri Ritchlin, and Carol Rolland: Your talents are responsible for retaining the vital elements of these mystical stories. Your uplifting personalities made the work fun for me. I couldn't have done *The Spirit of a Woman* without you. I am rich having each one of you in my life.

Contributing artist Nichola Moss: Thank you for sharing your artwork for the cover and interior of this book and for sharing your sacred stories with me.

May your hopeful images continue to bless others at www.nicholart.com.

My incredible publisher, Jeffrey Goldman of Santa Monica Press, is a blessing in my life. It was meant to be that we were brought together by synchronistic events. I am grateful for your many gifts and talents that guided the direction of this book. It is a joy to experience your creativity and passion for what you do.

About the Editor

TERRY LÁSZLÓ-GOPADZE is a licensed marriage and family therapist. She has become known to her audiences for her combination of humor, compassion, and courage as both a storyteller and a listener of stories. Terry also ran personal development workshops and groups in West Los Angeles for women, singles, and adolescents. She later expanded this work to include such diverse groups as cancer patients, Alcoholics Anonymous, university students, women's groups, and health centers. Offering workshops on storytelling, shamanism, forgiveness, courage, intuition, healing, and creating destiny has been her passion and joy.

Gathering sacred stories, and her own mystical journey, inspires her to share the many paths to Spirit with others. She lives in Del Mar, California, with her husband Lee, and is the happiest when her son Paul is home from college.

Please join our storytelling network and visit Terry and the authors at: www.womens-spirit.com and www.TheSpiritofaWomanBook.com.